The Formation of a Lay Apostle

The Formation of a Lay Apostle

Francis N. Wendell, O.P.

AROUCA
PRESS

Originally published in 1954 by The Third Order of St. Dominic, NYC.

New Edition © Arouca Press 2023

All rights reserved:
No part of this book may be reproduced or transmitted,
in any form or by any means, without permission

Cover image (Ade Bethune, "I am the good shepherd: I know mine
and mine know me.") courtesy of Archives and Special Collections,
St. Catherine University, St. Paul, Minnesota.

Cover design by Julian Kwasniewski
Layout by Allison Merrick

ISBN: 978-1-990685-45-3

Arouca Press
PO Box 55003
Bridgeport PO
Waterloo, ON N2J 3G0
Canada
www.aroucapress.com
Send inquiries to info@aroucapress.com

CENSORES ORDINIS:
Norbert F. Georges, O.P.
Richard E. Vahey, O.P.

IMPRIMI POTEST:
T. S. McDermott, O.P., S.T.M.
Prior Provincialis

NIHIL OBSTAT:
John M. A Fearns, S.T.D.
Censor Librorum

IMPRIMATUR:
✠ Francis Cardinal Spellman

May 9, 1954

TO MY MOTHER AND FATHER
In gratitude

Contents

Preface to the Second Edition (1954)

THIS BOOK IS OVER TEN YEARS OLD. A lot of water has gone over the dam in those ten years. Ten years ago the lay apostolate was virtually unknown in our country. Ten years of experimentation, of failure, of measured and limited success has led us to a point where now at least the terms no longer have to be defined. Almost everyone now knows what is meant by the lay apostolate. Catholic Action is a term that has become fairly accepted. More and more lay people and more and more priests and Bishops have come to see the necessary role and the function of the laity in the Church of the atomic age. This is an effort to bring this book up to date. It prompts us to put out a second edition and what is really a third printing. A couple of the chapters are basically unchanged; two ("I Am The Church" and "Queen of the Apostles") have been added. Most of them, however, are revised and thoroughly revised to bring one up to the situation as we see it today—ten years later.

FRANCIS N. WENDELL, O.P.
Feast of The Purification
February 2, 1954

CHAPTER ONE

A Lay Apostle—
Who, What and Where

In every age the Church has needed and employed the laity. Someone recently remarked: "This Catholic Church, it's a wonderful organization—you find it everywhere. I saw it on a little island in the South Pacific during the last war. I meet it in New York and I come across it on the broad plains of Kansas. It's organized as no other organization on the face of the earth. Pope, Cardinals, Archbishops, Bishops, Priests and Glory be to God, they are now organizing the laity." Yes, it is true. The problems of the modern day have demanded an increase and an organization, formal or informal, of the laity; souls—all kinds of souls—who are devoting themselves to the mission of the Church. The possibilities, the fields of the lay apostolate, are almost unlimited. The past five Popes, our present Pope Pius XII, not only urge but plead for this apostolate. Countries like Belgium, France, Holland talk in terms of 25, 30 years of lay apostolic history, of well-trained, well-regulated organizations, youth, married people, farmers; all have answered the call of the modern Popes.

The United States of America like some other countries has been slower to enter the formal lay apostolate field. Yet, work has been going on here almost as long; perhaps not as clearly defined, but it has been progressing. The Legion of Mary is well established in many parts of this country. Father Judge's Outer Cenacle of the Trinitarians is established in well over a hundred places in various parts of the United States—particularly the East, the South. Friendship Houses have increased. The Catholic Worker Movement has its farms, its houses of hospitality, its followers. The Young Christian Worker Movement is established from coast to coast—from San Diego and San Francisco to New York, Brooklyn and Manchester, New Hampshire. The Young Christian Student Movement has developed gradually in high schools and colleges. The Grail has a school of the apostolate in Loveland, Ohio, as well as several centers in various parts of this country. The Christian Family Movement has had a wider diffusion here than in any other country of the world.

Literature is now available. Whereas once it was extremely sparse, today it is comparatively easy to obtain.

What is the lay apostolate? What is a lay apostle? Very simply the lay apostle, as the term indicates, is a lay person engaged in some apostolic work. That leaves him with a broad field indeed. Pope Pius XII has insisted on the breadth of the apostolate and warned against any exclusivism and narrowness of any particular group or form of the apostolate. Gone are the days of the arguments is this or that Catholic Action, the interminable discussions about "the mandate" of the Bishop. These belong to the experts. Let them take care of it. Briefly there are innumerable phases of the lay apostolate, all important. There are many organizations within the lay apostolic program, there are many souls engaged in apostolic work "on their own," for example the Christopher type of apostolate. These too are lay apostles and as such stand in need of certain definite training and formation. This formation which must be accomplished is especially the work of the priest. We might also mention, however, in

3

passing that the best form of the apostolate would seem to be the organized apostolate, since the enemy, as Pope Pius XI so frequently pointed out, is also organized. Here the Church will find its most valuable auxiliaries and members.

THE WHAT

The lay apostle has a double function to accomplish. The first, like that of every other human being, is his own sanctification. The second is his, what we might call, external mission, which is the sanctification and the salvation of his fellowman, carrying with it, today more than ever before, the other twin function of the apostolizing of social institutions, (more about that later). Both functions are vital. To neglect one is to strip one's self of all rightful claim of this title "lay apostle." It still is true that no one can give what he does not have, and that the one who attempts to be an instrument in the sanctification of others while neglecting himself is an enigma, and sometimes somewhat of a pest. He may accomplish a certain amount of good, even a great deal of good for a time, but there will hardly be any lasting spiritual effects from his apostolic work if indeed it can be called apostolic at all. The God of good works must never be deserted for the good works of God. "What doth it profit a man if he gain the whole world and suffer the loss of his soul?"

Above all, then, the lay apostle must be a man with an interior life. This does not imply sanctity before he can enter the arena. No one says he must be fully developed spiritually. At the start there are no full-blown lay apostles. There must, however, be a minimum, a beginning, and that is the *desire* to love God. Then, indeed, the very external work of the apostolate itself can be and should be one of the means of the lay apostle's sanctification. Formation and apostolate go hand in hand—the effort to serve the Church shows one the need for grace and grace in turn inspires one to serve the Church. The second function of the lay apostle is the one that is most frequently misunderstood and misinterpreted. That is the function of sanctification and salvation of one's neighbor and the penetration of social institutions with the spirit and love of Christ. One must never limit the lay apostolate to helping with the priestly apostolate. Sometimes this is necessary, even vital; the laborers among the priestly apostles are few and the fields still white for the harvest. But this is the priestly apostolate being assisted by the lay apostolate.

There is a specifically lay apostolate. The apostolate of the factory, the workbench, the office, the classroom, the home, the marriage, the family. This is the layman's field, he works here, lives here, dies here. If a new social order is to be re-constructed, and the modern Popes have certainly provided the blueprint, it is going to be constructed by lay people. This is their field. Priests must help them accomplish their *lay* apostolate. Indeed they cannot do it without the help of priests, but priests cannot do it for them. Priests must help them, form them, train them, but they must do the work, live the life.

"The apostle of a working man must be another working man," as Pope Pius XI said in *Quadragesimo Anno*. No one else can accomplish this task. He will not accept help from lawyers or doctors or professional men. He will accept help sometimes from the priest, frequently not even from him. But he will always respect and understand another worker. This is the famous apostolate of like by like—a very important psychological factor in modern life and in the modern apostolate; it can be overstressed but frequently it is underestimated.

The apostolic role of the layman must be also to penetrate the institutions of his society. He cannot be rescuing others and then at the same time letting them fall back into a world where business practices, governmental restrictions, economic and social upheavals strangle the very life blood out of them. The lay apostle must be concerned with morality in government, in business, in daily life, he must be concerned with press, radio and, now, television. To use the famous old example—the fish are swimming in polluted water, he must not merely dip them out for a breath of fresh air or some fresh water, he must change the water, the environment, the *milieu*, as the French put it.

From all this one can see the vast scope of the lay apostolate, the tremendous ideas envisioned by the modern Popes notably Leo XIII, Pius XI and Pius XII. Pius XI said that he had come to his definition of Catholic Action "not without Divine inspiration." More and more one is beginning to see how Divine and how necessary it really is.

WHERE?

Some years ago a movie came out from England entitled, "I Know Where I'm Going." There was a theme song that ran though this movie with a very haunting melody that read "I know where I'm going and I know who goes with me." The apostle must know where he is going and with whom he is going. He is leading toward sanctity—nothing more

7

and nothing less. For him to aim at anything less would be a fatal mistake. "This is the Will of God," St. Paul said, "your sanctification."

He is also going with someone, with Christ and through Mary. Christ and Mary become his companions through life into eternity. "I have loved thee with an everlasting love." But he is not going alone. He is going with others—with other workers, other students, other friends, members of his own family. A Christian, Pope Pius XI used to say, is by nature an apostle. It is sheer folly to think of a Christian going to God alone. "Other sheep I have that are not of this fold, them also must I bring." The whole world belongs to God—people and even things—the City of God and the city of man are united—the eternal and the temporal order, the field of work and the area of the sanctuary melt together. Man is not an angel, he dwells in the world, his environment is part of his life, his work and his family and his recreation are all areas that must be affected by Our Lord's Incarnation.

There is today an alarming numerical insufficiency of the clergy in many countries of the world. Even in our country we might be surprised to realize the shortage of priests. In a diocese, a small diocese of northern Michigan, 51 priests are saying three Masses every Sunday. Some years ago a priest made a survey of this country, particularly concentrating on the South and Southwest. He termed this area "no priest land," for he found that one-third of the counties of the United States never had a resident priest within their borders.

But even if there were sufficient priests there would be a tremendous need for the lay apostolate. Even where the Church is accepted and allowed to operate, as in our own country, there is a problem. For the Church has been expelled from every country in the world in this sense—*that she has been confined more and more to the Sanctuary*. She has been told that she may operate; but within the field of the specifically religious. There is needed then a philosophy of presence that can be exercised only by lay people since they are present in and are of the world.

Obviously to exercise this apostolate effectively, lay people must be formed, they must grow in holiness. What, me a saint! Yes, you, Joe Doakes in the local factory and Helen Smith of the Telephone Company. You must become saints, not in a cloister, not by way of an artificial holiness but a whole holiness, an integrated holiness, a lay holiness. The layman and the lay woman must become holy by being good workers, faithful and competent, a good wife, a dedicated

9

doctor, a proficient lawyer, an apostle to other workers, other lawyers, other doctors, other families.

It is the burden of this booklet to show how the formation of this lay apostle can be accomplished. The priest is formed for many years in the seminary, the layman is to be formed for many years in and through his daily life.

CHAPTER TWO

"I Am the Church"

L ay people generally think of themselves as belonging to the Church. When they begin to get the concept that they *are* the Church they begin to be lay apostles. The doctrine of the Mystical Body of Christ is at the very heart of the lay apostolate. Christ is still living in the world in another body, it is true, a mystical, a mysterious body. The Catholic Church is not just an organization but an organism, a living body, a body with life that is Divine.

"I am the vine, you are the branches." . . . "I came that you might have life, and have it more abundantly." . . . "I am . . . the Life." The impact of these ideas is tremendous. Christ lives in me, a layman, an ordinary worker, or as a man said to me just recently, "just imagine, someone asked my advice and I am only a taxicab driver." There is revolution here, revolution in the sense that one's life begins to be important. *Christ living in me*, this is revolution. "We need not fear the revolution, we *are* the revolution."

With all this there come two clear, distinct revelations. First, I am related to Christ, He is the Head of the Body and I am a member of His Body, the Church. He is my friend, I walk and talk with Him as Adam walked and talked with God in the cool and shade of the evening as a friend. The doctrine of grace. Friendship with God—playing, as someone has said, in a league that is over one's head.

The second realization for the layman is almost as important. I am related to all the other members of the body. We are all one in Christ Jesus our Head. I am related to Bill Brown who sits next to me at work and Bill Murphy who sits on top of me in the subway. I am related to the cab driver whose name I see written above his license, Solomon Levy. They are all members of this Body either actually or potentially, the good and the bad. I must love them all. The good I must love for their goodness which they get from Christ. The bad I must love for their need. The Jew I must love because God made him and he might some day enjoy membership in the

Body. There is no color in the Mystical Body, the yellow, the red, the black and the white are all one in Christ.

The discovery of this doctrine opens up a tremendous field for the lay apostle. He begins to see—I am responsible for others because I am related to them. I have the greatest gift in the world, actual membership in Christ's Body, but the Body must grow and I must help it to grow. Therein lies my apostolate. I must work not as the priest, not preaching, not hearing little confessions or giving short homilies, but I must exercise my apostolate as a layman, doing all the things that I am required to do as a layman. Yet it is not my apostolate but His, Christ's. He uses me as an instrument to fill up what is wanting in the Passion of Christ. His love present in my soul will redeem souls *now*, in this very year, just as He redeemed them on the first Good Friday.

FORMATION THROUGH ACTION

Lay people cannot, like the priest, go away to a seminary for extensive training. Nor should they. They must be trained where they are. Indeed to take them away, certainly for any considerable length of time, from the environment runs the risk of producing "hothouse apostles," people who have lost contact with the environment, people who have become so different that they are no longer accepted.

It is for this reason that the principle long advocated by the Young Christian Worker Movement (Jocist in France and Belgium), the principle of formation through action, is so important.

Lay people are not to become holy in spite of their life but in and through their life. The Sacrament of their apostolate, Confirmation, is not a Sacrament of passive resistance but of active apostolate. The Holy Spirit wants to help form Christ in laymen so that Christ may continue His work through them. This implies action, not any action it is true, but intelligent, generous Christian action, active love. "What is needed," said His Holiness Pope Pius XII in 1949, in speaking of the Young Christian Workers, "is the active presence in factories and work places, of pioneers who are fully conscious of their double vocation—as Christians and workers—and who are bent on assuming their responsibilities to the full, knowing neither peace nor rest until they have transformed the environment of their lives to the demands of the Gospel. The Church, by this positive, constructive work, will be able to extend her life-giving action to the millions of souls for whom she has a maternal and ardent solicitude."

The lay person must be apprised of the fact that it is in the very accomplishing of the ordinary things of life that he becomes holy. The traveling to work, the making of the baby's formula, the rendering of an honest day's work, all these are the warp and woof out of which lay sanctity is woven.

CHAPTER THREE

Time in One's Life

Any life to be effective must be ordered. Even in those who live a purely natural life, and who attain a purely natural degree of success, we always find order. Therefore we have a right to look for a certain amount of order in the life of one who is trying to live a supernatural life. There are so many opportunities and occasions for distraction inherent in the very nature of the lay apostle's life. He lives in the world, he works in the world, he plays in the world, he carries on his, if you will, ministry, in the world *and yet he is not of the world*. His position under the very best of circumstances is precarious. Considered from a purely natural point of view, he is like the tightrope walker performing before a hostile crowd in a heavy wind without the aid of the traditional umbrella. Supernaturally, of course, it is a different matter. Here he is like Christ bringing beauty and order into a world damaged by sin. But that is just the point—to bring Christ, the supernatural, into the lay apostle's life.

Religious institutes have the answer to an ordered life for their members in their approved rule and constitutions. The religious superior represents Christ to the religious. Yet this the lay person lacks—he has no one and no rule of life, unless he be a member of a Third Order, to guide him. True he has the Commandments of God and the precepts of the Church. He also has the duties of his state in life and for the layman these are extremely important. *It is in the prudent exercise of the duties of his state in life that the layman is chiefly to find his holiness.*

What is the practical solution? Is a schedule or horarium practical for the lay person? The answer to this is yes and no. Yes, because some order must be found and fostered in the lay life, at least a minimum. No, because the schedule of the lay apostle will differ from person to person according to time and circumstances. In practice it is up to the individual to draw up some kind of a practical schedule and then by trial and error to work it out successfully.

Some lay groups indicate minimum requirements for their members. Others do not. Much of this is a matter of practical experience and experimentation. It is something that should be discussed with one's confessor or spiritual director. A consideration of a certain few things, we think, is essential.

THE HEART OF THE MATTER

There are a few practices that are essential for a balanced and ordered lay life. We set them down here with a brief comment on each one but will return to them in more detail later.

1. *Daily Mass When and If Possible.* This cannot always be a starting point, it is a goal. The lay apostle should not just go to Mass because someone says he should, but should try and find out why he should attend Mass daily. This is not a formula. This is the heart of Christianity. The death of Christ renewed and re-presented, nothing else could be more important. This is the very heart and cause of the apostolate.

2. *Daily or Frequent Communion.* This is a completion of the Mass, the Food of the soul, the Bread of Life.

Holy Communion is a part of Mass and should be received whenever possible.

3. *Prayer.* Conversation with the One that the lay apostle loves and is serving must grow from the ordinary vocal prayer up and through meditation or mental prayer, a *sine qua non* of the spiritual life, to a habit of constant prayer and eventually to the highest forms of prayer if God should so bless the soul.

4. *Reading—Spiritual, Social and/or Intellectual.* The lay apostle's mind must be fed not only by the truths of the faith through good spiritual reading but also through a reading of the social doctrines of the Church. This is a feeder for prayer. Above all other forms of reading a regular perusal of Sacred Scripture comes first.

5. *The Choice and Intelligent Use of a Regular Confessor and Director.* This is not only in accord with the mind of the Church, her saints, doctors and spiritual writers but is also a dictate of good common sense. *The man who directs himself follows a fool.* This direction should be fairly regular depending on person and circumstances. Weekly confession for a lay apostle would certainly seem to be in order. In the case of the

young, direction should also be quite frequent. Many groups likewise have quarterly a day of recollection, some even monthly. So important is this practice of retreat that Dom Chautard in his invaluable little booklet, "The Soul of the Apostolate," ventures the opinion that the monthly retreat is "almost indispensable to the man engaged in good works."

The essentials are lined up and adapted to the particular layman. He must then make an effort to bring some sort of order into his life. However, there is in every lay life the element of unpredictability and for this reason his so-called "schedule" must be both *flexible* and *inflexible*. This is not a contradiction. His schedule must be flexible for the simple reason that the duties of his state in life continually bend and change. As to his apostolate, souls are involved and souls have a way of needing help at various and odd moments. The Holy Spirit breathes where He will and is not subject to the caprice of a man-made horarium. A lay apostle who would adhere so closely to a schedule that he would pass up an opportunity to perform a true, vital or necessary act of charity would in reality be failing in his vocation. St. Thomas Aquinas, mystic and busy scholar that he was, begins one of his letters: "Tonight I have given up my prayer in order to write to you."

There are certain people whose idea of a horarium is limited to a neatly typed piece of paper that has been plastered on a wall and then promptly forgotten. Theirs is not a flexible schedule but an elastic one that theoretically stretches on into infinity; practically, such a schedule reaches the point of non-existence. These people need an inflexible element in their life in order to achieve any order at all.

A very important quality that should be found in a lay apostle's schedule is practicality. Recreation for example is important and must have its place. The whole thing must be balanced. Anyone who has attempted to bring order into his life admits the necessity of adhering habitually and daily to a certain few habits. A definite rising hour practically adhered to might almost be said to be the crux of an ordered life. The retiring hour also is an important factor but of the two, a regular and an early rising hour would seem to be more important.

There is an almost infallible gauge as to the practicality of a scheduled life. If curtailments, dispensations, interruptions, become habitual, then something is definitely wrong. Either the schedule is poorly planned, impossible, or the lay apostle has allowed his work or some part of his life to get out of focus, thereby hindering the perfection of the whole. In either case the matter should be presented and discussed with the spiritual director and necessary adjustments made without delay.

CHAPTER FOUR

Spiritual Direction of the Lay Apostle

While spiritual direction is not an absolute necessity for personal sanctification, it is nevertheless, one of the normal means for advancing in the ways of God. As far as the lay apostle is concerned it can be stated quite flatly that for him or her a spiritual director is an obvious and positive necessity when available. After all, God established His Church as a hierarchical society that was to work for the sanctification of souls, as Tanquerey points out, "Through submission to the Sovereign Pontiff and Bishops in things external, and to confessors in things internal." If this be true for all men it must be doubly true for those who have entered the arena of the lay apostolate.

Pope Leo XIII, arguing in the same vein, says: "God in His Infinite Providence has decreed that men for the most part should be saved by men." This has been the constant teaching of practically all the saints and doctors of the Church from the very earliest times. For anyone (but for the lay apostle, in particular) to say that there is no need for spiritual direction is to invite disaster. Speaking of those who scorn direction Pope Leo XIII again says: "Those who reject it, assuredly do so rashly and at their peril."

From a purely psychological point of view a spiritual director is a necessity. No man is a good judge of his own case. In spiritual matters, as in other matters, there is a tendency to be satisfied, to relax and say "not bad" or "pretty good." Nothing of course can be more fatal in the spiritual order. High ideals get imperceptibly lowered until they are no longer the same ideals. They are now easily attainable. The goal is no longer in sight. It is possessed. There is very little more to do than just hold on to it. The flaws in such reasoning processes and the defects in the lay apostle's conduct would of course be apparent to the mind and eyes of a good director. Moreover, he could (and he should) insist on higher goals and ever greater strivings. If, as St. Bernard says, "the measure to love God is to love Him without measure," then there can be no question of our attaining the goal here on earth. We must always strive higher.

CONFESSOR-DIRECTOR

There is a difference between a confessor and a spiritual director. A confessor, by reason of his office, seems to deal directly and immediately with sin and therefore only indirectly with the positive side of the spiritual life; the director on the other hand deals directly and immediately with the positive side of the spiritual life, such as prayer, virtue, mortification, etc., and only indirectly with sin. It might surprise some people that confessor and director can be two distinct persons. St. Francis de Sales, for example, was the spiritual director of a great many people but not their confessor. Ordinarily, however, and practically it would seem to be best that where possible the one priest fulfill both offices. For, after all, to direct intelligently the priest must know the actual state and condition of the soul under his care and this is best learned in the Sacrament of Penance where the soul lies stripped of any false adornments.

It goes without saying that spiritual direction is not a matter of hide-and-go-seek. The lay apostle must exert every effort to make himself known to his director, his bad points as well as his good ones. There must not be any of what someone was quoted as saying, "I go regularly to one priest except when I commit a mortal sin." Strangely enough there are some souls who either through false humility, timidity or reserve, make it very difficult for the director to have any set judgment as to their spiritual condition. They are like those people who go to a doctor and then quite steadfastly refuse to tell him what is ailing them.

It is extremely important that the priest know the lay life. This is not a matter of a weekly pious exhortation or a monthly one, or of any at all. This is a matter of the confessor-director applying the moral principles to the specific daily lay life of the penitent. It is, for example, most important that the director understand the situation of John Smith who works in a local bank and has a take-home pay of $46.20, along with a family of four children. The director must come to know what it means under these circumstances to be sorely tempted to practice artificial limitation of a family in such unjust economic difficulties. He must also come to understand what it means to be a human being like Mary Jones engaged for a year and a half and yet unable to find a place in our society where she and her husband-to-be can live and bring up a family. He must understand what it means to work in a factory and be surrounded by obscene language, to work in a restaurant and to suffer the indignities to which a young waitress is frequently subjected. This is the lay life. The priest cannot possibly understand it unless the lay person brings it to him and makes it known to him.

On the other hand there are lay people who talk too much, the loquacious type, those given over to pious (sometimes impious) prattle. These volunteer information in abundance, some of it relevant, most of it irrelevant. These are like that other type of person who, when asked "how are you?" leave the listener aghast at the long list of their illnesses. Priests are very busy people, their time is precious—it must not be wasted.

THE INTELLIGENT CHOICE OF A DIRECTOR

The lay apostle's first task then is to find a good spiritual director. This necessarily involves a matter of judgment and is something that must not be done haphazardly. Certain qualities of mind and soul must be found in the person who is to take upon himself the difficult and frightening task of fashioning the soul of another human being. What are these qualities? They can be ascertained by some careful thinking.

Certainly the lay apostle has a right to look for *knowledge* in his prospective director. This means not only the technical knowledge of ascetical and mystical theology but also sound judgment and prudence, both natural and supernatural. The director on his part should never forget (nor should the one directed) that the Supreme Director of the human soul is the Holy Ghost Who operates in the soul by means of His supernatural virtues and gifts. The human director must become the instrument of the Holy Spirit. One of his chief tasks is to try to distinguish for his penitent the difference between the inspirations of the Holy Ghost and those of the imagination—a task that is not always easy.

The great Carmelite mystic, St. Teresa of Avila, had some very definite opinions on this matter of a director's knowledge. She learned from bitter experience the danger of unwise spiritual direction. For many years she suffered at the hands of directors who, while they may have been pious, were not particularly learned. The great Spanish mystic was very specific in warning against this combination in a director.

Among the qualities of soul that the lay apostle should look for in the director there might be mentioned *personal holiness, patience, humility, generosity* (particularly with regard to time), *firmness* and finally *approachableness*. Perhaps these could be summed up by saying that the director should be a man blessed with an abundance of *supernatural charity* which will manifest itself in a paternal affection for the spiritual children that go to him.

The natural qualities of *firmness* and *approachableness* have a special practical value. The director's charity certainly does not mean weakness. He can and he must be firm, especially at times, with the patients. As Tanquerey wisely warns he must "not allow himself to be directed by them."

As for *approachableness*, that is a quality not shared by everyone but a quality that is a great help in drawing souls to Christ. There are certain people to whom almost anyone can speak with ease while there are others, perhaps more gifted in mind and soul, to whom many have great difficulty in "opening up." Very often this difficulty is more apparent than real, and sometimes persistence helps one "open up." Experience, however, does show that this idea of approachableness is something that enters almost unconsciously and necessarily into the choice of a director.

DIFFICULTY IN FINDING A DIRECTOR

Saint Gregory the Great says: "The direction of souls is the art of arts." The difficulty in finding a suitable spiritual director just about bears out the saint's statement. Almost any group of lay apostles to whom this question of spiritual direction is proposed inevitably come back with: "Yes, all that is true. But where are we going to find these directors who have the time, the ability or the inclination to give this direction?" Their question cannot be brushed aside as an excuse for their own spiritual inadequacy—*for these lay people are in deadly earnest.* At the same time it should be noted that this problem is not a new one. St. Vincent Ferrer, the great Dominican preacher of the 14th century, is said to have remarked in effect: "I search everywhere and I cannot find a suitable spiritual director." All of which does not answer the question . . .

The only answer, of course, is that suitable spiritual directors exist and the only thing for the lay apostle to do is to search until one is found. That means just that—*search*. Mistakes will be made, that is to be expected, along with disappointments. However, persistence is important. It is the effort to find direction that God expects, not the success in finding it. Meanwhile God in His mercy will take care of that soul who is sincerely seeking this normal means of holiness.

As a matter of fact, the good director is soon known by reputation. Word gets around that he is proficient in this matter, and souls, especially in our day, actually hungry for the spiritual life, flock to him in abundance. Such a priest is just about literally swamped with work but at the same time, he is more than willing to sacrifice himself in order that these precious, chosen souls be brought closer to Christ.

Once such a director is found the lay apostle should thank God that the search is over and realize that for him the work has really begun. He must use the director intelligently and prudently, neither demanding too much of his time nor too little. Of course, a great deal of the regulating of the direction depends upon the discretion of the priest. The success of the direction depends upon both the cooperation of the priest and the lay apostle with the graces so freely bestowed upon the human soul by an infinitely generous God.

CHAPTER FIVE

The Holy Eucharist and the Lay Apostle

The Holy Eucharist is a sacrifice and a sacrament. The sacrifice, Holy Mass, is directly concerned with the worship and glory of God; the sacrament, which St. Thomas calls the greatest of all the sacraments because it contains in Itself God Himself, Holy Communion, is directly concerned with man's sanctification. Both, of course, are closely connected. Both, in some way, glorify and worship God; both, in some way, sanctify man. Holy Communion is an integral part of Holy Mass. After the priest receives Communion the Sacrifice of the Mass is integrally complete.

The degree of the lay apostle's spiritual and apostolic life can be measure by the degree of his Eucharistic life. Our Lord promised that he that would eat of this Bread would live forever. Indeed, Dom Chautard in "The Soul of the Apostolate" says: "The good results obtained by the apostolate correspond invariably to the degree of Eucharistic life acquired by the apostle." That this must necessarily be so is not hard to see. Our Lord Himself returned to this theme time and time again: "As the branch cannot bear fruit of itself . . . so neither can you, unless you abide in Me. He that abideth in Me and I in him, the same beareth much fruit."

THE SACRIFICE OF THE MASS

Here is Calvary all over again. This is Calvary represented and reenacted. For here Christ, as on Calvary, is at once the Priest and the Victim. Here again He offers Himself as Priest to the Heavenly Father, here He is offered as Victim to that same Father. He offers Himself not alone but now with His mystical members.

Herein is the great lesson for the lay apostle regarding the Mass—the Mass is something he does along with Christ. The saintly Pope Pius X once wrote: "The primary and the indispensable source of the true Christian spirit is to be found in the active participation of the laity in the Sacred Mysteries (the Mass)." The Mass is not something that the lay apostle watches or attends, it is something that he does. "Active participation"—something that he does with Christ the Priest and Christ the Victim. Christ once again stands on Calvary and offers Himself to the Heavenly Father but this time He offers Himself with this young doctor, this old lawyer, this little child, this grimy, tired worker. Not only that, but this same doctor, same lawyer, same child, same worker is united to Christ the Victim and *is offered* to the Father with Christ. Here is Christian worship at its peak. An infinite act, with infinite value. This is the Mass. The great moment of that Mass, the lay apostle comes to learn, is the moment of Consecration when through the separate consecration of the bread and wine Christ's death is mystically enacted for our times. He comes to learn that it is truly the Mass that matters.

A MASS-CENTERED DAY AND LIFE

Unfortunately all lay people cannot attend daily Mass. This is certainly understandable. Yet even among those who cannot be there, there seems to be an almost instinctive, or rather, inspired, recognition as to the importance of daily Mass. Once a soul has begun to live the Christian and the apostolic life in real earnest, the Holy Sacrifice of the Mass takes on a new meaning, even though perhaps for a long time that meaning remains somewhat confused in his mind. The Mass looms larger and larger on his horizon. Daily attendance gradually becomes almost a necessity. A day begun without Mass is a day begun without the Eucharistic Christ and therefore lacking in something, or should we say Someone. Each morning the Mass becomes more and more of a reality until gradually the lay apostle would no more think of beginning his day without the Mass than he would think of writing a letter without paper.

The lay apostle comes gradually to recognize the fact that the Sacrifice of the Mass is intimately connected with his own redemption, the forgiveness of his personal sins, the redemption of the world. Where would I be, where would I be going without Calvary? What despair would there be in the world if Christ had not purchased its redemption? Of what value would be my apostolate without Christ's death? Would there be an apostolate at all? Of what value would be my life?

He begins to understand the meaning of *Ite Missa Est.* "Go, this is the Mass." You have participated in the greatest act of worship that the world has ever known, the death of Jesus Christ; go out now and live it. Bring it back to your workbench, to your office, to the telephone company. *Ite Missa Est*, live the Mass in every part of life with every soul you meet, with the man that sits next to you on the bus, with the boss who harasses you at work, with a member of your own family with whom you have so much difficulty getting along.

At the same time the lay apostle realizes his own lack of knowledge of this great mystery, and with this realization comes the desire to know more about Christ the Victim and Christ the Priest. Knowledge of the Holy Sacrifice must of necessity become essential, for love and appreciation are always preceded by knowledge. To this end the sincere lay apostle will study the Mass, make a determined effort to grasp as best he can its history, dogma, meaning. That is why study and discussion clubs especially devoted to the Mass are in order. However, these must be made interesting, visual. Dialogue Masses, Dry Masses, the seeing and feeling and touching of the vestments and instruments of the Holy Sacrifice (when and where allowed) help a great deal. That is why, too, in the specialized movements of Catholic Action especially in this country, a short study of the Liturgy has become a part of their weekly meetings. A true appreciation of the Mass takes much time and grace.

DAILY OR FREQUENT COMMUNION

Holy Communion completes the Mass; indeed if the priest should not receive Holy Communion the Mass would be an incomplete Sacrifice. Here the lay apostle should unite himself with Our Blessed Lord. Only the priest has the power of bringing Our Lord's Body and Blood, Soul and Divinity on the altar. But all are invited to partake of the Banquet. "Take ye and eat."

It is not at all strange then that a lover of Christ should want to be Eucharistically with Him frequently or even daily. Indeed, the opposite would be strange. Each time that a lay apostle attends Mass he should try to receive Our Lord and if he attends daily he should therefore receive daily. This is the moment of greatest intimacy when, as Pope Pius XII pointed out in his Encyclical on the Mystical Body, Our Lord "longs to converse with the soul."

Holy Communion works certain effects in the lay

apostle's soul just as in the soul of anyone else. First and foremost the reception of the Holy Eucharist brings about a union between Christ and the lay apostle. Love always seeks union and here the union is *real*, that is the real physical Body and Blood of Christ, His Soul and Divinity, are united with man.

Holy Communion also becomes the food that sustains the lay apostle's spiritual life just as natural food sustains his physical life. There is special need for sustenance in the apostolate and the best assurance of spiritual growth is to be found right here. "My flesh is meat indeed, and my blood is drink indeed." The Sacraments produce grace of themselves. In all the other Sacraments man receives the grace of God; in the Holy Eucharist he receives the God of grace, God Himself.

This Sacrament, according to St. Thomas, remits venial sin and the temporal punishment due to sin. This of course is an excellent argument against those who say they are "not good enough" to receive daily. Who is? Holy Communion helps make one better.

Holy Communion is also a source of spiritual joy. Joy is an effect of charity and here in this Sacrament is Charity at white heat, Love Itself.

The lay apostle has the normal temptations of every human being with perhaps a few others thrown in as a result of his engaging in an apostolate. Again the frequent reception of Holy Communion will be a valid defense against temptation. In the matter of overcoming temptations of the flesh, there is no greater guarantee of success in the supernatural order. Souls that have been subjected to the most furious assaults against the angelic virtue of purity have found their salvation in the frequent and even daily reception of the Holy Eucharist.

Finally, Holy Communion is a pledge of the lay apostle's future glory. We have the word of Christ Himself for this: "If any man eat of this bread, he shall live forever." This is the crowning glory, as it were, of Holy Communion, the promise of God that the union begun on earth shall last even in eternity. Love seeks union. Love has found it here eternally.

We must also see Holy Communion as not just an individual and intimate relationship between the soul and Our Lord but also as a social Sacrament wherein all souls gather round a banquet table and draw closer to Christ and thereby closer to one another. The same Christ that is received in one is received in the other, or could be received there in that person. The effects of Holy Communion therefore should be shown among men in their relationship with one another, in society as a whole, in the affairs of men as well as God. Many millions received Him this morning, many more millions have never tasted of this Banquet. By uniting myself with Our Lord I unite myself with the millions that have and the millions that have not, I become a little closer to all of them. "With Christ for others, with others for Christ!"

There are many thousands of souls in the world today who are on fire with the love of Christ; but they do not know what to do about it. Each morning they throng our churches in what appears to be an ever increasing number, especially of young women and some young men who daily approach the Sacrificial Banquet. Many of them undergo great sacrifices in order to receive Christ each day. But they want to do even more. The love of Christ is consuming them, they are looking, often vainly, for an outlet for their apostolic zeal. Here is where the social aspect of Christianity should operate. These souls should be the special object of the zeal of confirmed lay apostles. *These are potential, if not actual, lay apostles*. One word, one smile, one conversation may reveal to these souls the outlet that they have been seeking. The confirmed lay apostles and these potential ones have a common ground on which to build their friendship, the

Eucharistic Christ. It is definitely up to the experienced lay apostle to introduce these other souls to some apostolic way of life. Goodness never remains stationary. It must, of necessity, diffuse itself. One of the signs of good lay apostles is their desire and their effort to draw other souls into the serious business of restoring all things in Christ.

A WORD ABOUT PREPARATION AND THANKSGIVING

Nine times out of ten when people complain of apparently fruitless Communions, the source of the trouble is to be found in either a poor preparation or thanksgiving, or both. The lay apostle's preparation before Holy Communion should certainly consist in acts of humility, "Lord, I am not worthy," and acts of desire to be united to our Sacramental Lord, "With desire I have desired to eat this pasch with you." The time allotted to this preparation must, of necessity, vary from person to person; but it certainly should never be a hit-and-miss affair or something that is entirely, or almost entirely, neglected.

As to thanksgiving, this is one of the most common problems of all. Here there should be found a colloquy, a conversation, between the soul and the Divine Guest. This is *the* propitious moment to pour out our love for Christ, to thank Him for His graces, to pray for those near and dear to us, to meet the problems of our apostolate, to beg the Divine Guest for the gifts we need most. This is common, ordinary courtesy, to say the least. This Thanksgiving, like the preparation, should be as fervent and as long as we can reasonably make it.

CHAPTER SIX

The Prayer of the Lay Apostle

People who are in love delight in telling one another about it. So true is this that very often we find them, for this very reason, getting on the nerves of their relatives and friends. "What are you two talking about *now?*" they ask, or, "Don't you two ever get tired?" Strangely enough, with or without opposition, the lovers just go on talking (repeat themselves they will certainly do), and as for getting tired, that state somehow never overcomes them.

People who are in love with God delight in telling Him about it. So true is this that very often we find them also getting on the nerves of their relatives and friends. "Doesn't she ever get tired?" we hear them whisper, or, "What can

47

he possible be praying about *this* time?" they say in a tone that indicates at least mild irritation. But, strangely enough, with or without opposition, she goes blithely on with her prayers, and he never seems to lack something to pray for this time or any time.

Prayer is to the lay apostle what air is to breathing—he can't get along without it. Very early (although perhaps gradually) the lay apostle must come to realize the essential part prayer plays in his life and in his apostolate. This is the language of God and the apostle who is a lover of God must learn the language. The better he speaks God's language the better he loves God; the less he speaks it the less he loves God. It should be the lay apostle's aim to engage in what St. Augustine has defined as "familiar conversation with God," not occasionally or even frequently but, insofar as it is possible, constantly. The lay apostle, let us say this, is a potential saint and must not be content with the minimum in things spiritual. The sky is not the limit; it is just the beginning.

The lay apostle who neglects or sidetracks prayer is somewhat of a spiritual monstrosity. This is the very backbone of the apostolate. Without it "apostolic" work becomes more and more a matter of humanitarianism or even a cloak for personal vanity. The would-be apostle's shallowness becomes daily more evident until gradually those with whom he works find themselves repelled and he himself becomes disgusted with himself, discouraged and finally gives up the apostolate as an impossible task. It was not without reason that St. Augustine linked successful living and prayer. "He alone knows how to live well," he said, "who knows how to pray well." To which one might add, "and *vice versa.*"

VOCAL PRAYER

Vocal prayer is that type of prayer wherein the sentiments of the person are expressed through the organs of speech. It is a form of prayer that takes in the whole man, soul as well as body. All public prayer is necessarily vocal prayer. The Liturgy of the Church, for example, is vocal prayer. Any attempt to minimize this form of prayer is really a failure to understand the true nature of this most common form of God's language.

Besides the daily attendance at Mass the lay apostle can and should find many opportunities for vocal prayer. In the office, shop, factory, on the bus and in the living room there are countless opportunities for turning to God by way of short ejaculatory prayers and aspirations. Prayer is not something detachable. Man does not wear it like he wears his hat or his eyeglasses. Rather it is something that belongs to his very nature like his head or his spinal column. Hence it can be engaged in constantly. A Young Christian Worker in a noisy factory where the language was far from exemplary, on being questioned one time as to how long he went without being aware of God's Presence replied that sometimes he went as long as five minutes, never any more.

Our Lord said "Pray always." As a matter of fact this is not as hard as it may seem. All of man's acts can and should be a prayer. St. Thomas Aquinas in his Commentary on Romans says: "Man prays as long as he directs his whole life toward God." In his First Epistle to the Corinthians St. Paul puts it this way: "Whether you eat or drink or whatever else you do, do all to the glory of God."

The lay apostle must not be discouraged by the difficulties of this task. This is a matter of constant and sustained effort and, what is more important, a humble acknowledgment of one's own incapacity for such fidelity accompanied with a humble and sincere trust in the powerful grace of God. "I can do all things in Him who strengthens me."

Speaking about difficulties, there would seem to be two main ones in the matter of prayer. The first is the problem of distraction. The lay life is full of distraction. Lay people are in the world, immersed in it, sometimes surrounded by its very worst elements. It is not unlikely then that if the monk or the nun finds many distractions, the lay person will probably find more. The big question to settle here is "Are my distractions deliberate?" "How can I make them less deliberate?"

St. Thomas Aquinas has a very consoling doctrine for those who are pestered by distractions. He says that as long as the distractions are not deliberate they do not rob us of the merit of the prayer. In other words we get as much from the prayer as if we said it perfectly. Nor do they rob us of the efficacy of our prayer, the person for whom we pray gets as much. The only thing we lose, according to the Angelic Doctor, is the refreshment that normally should be ours as a result of praying. Indeed sometimes the very state of distraction, when it is indeliberate, is more meritorious than the prayer itself, by reason of the tremendous will that we have to exert in order to pray in the face of obstacles.

The second difficulty is the so-called difficulty of "dryness in prayer." Sometimes this is our own fault by reason of our distracted prayer, our distracted life, our sinfulness, our lukewarmness. Sometimes too this dryness is a gift of

God in disguise, testing us, purifying us, preparing us for an advance in the life of prayer. It is at this level that a spiritual director can render invaluable aid to the soul by helping that soul ascertain what is the cause of the dryness and how it should be dealt with.

MENTAL PRAYER

Besides vocal prayer there is also mental prayer, that prayer which is perfected by the internal acts of the mind and the will. We might say that every interior act of the mind or the will that unites man to God can be termed mental prayer. Authors list in this class such acts as reasoning, recollection, consideration, self-examination, the loving thought of God and contemplation—provided that all of these specific acts tend to unite man to God.

Sometimes the terms meditation and mental prayer are used interchangeably; sometimes, by certain authors, they are distinguished. Actually meditation refers more to the reasoned step-by-step consideration of things. Mental prayer is the broader term taking in this and other forms of prayer as we shall see later. The important thing to remember, however, is that the intellect and the will both play a great part in this form of prayer. Both are necessary. Someone has defined mental prayer as thinking about God with love. The last part, the love, the act or acts of the will is the more important part, though the first part, the thinking, is necessary at least in some way.

A lay apostle should be encouraged to spend maybe five or ten minutes each day at the beginning in this thinking about God with love. In the beginning he may need some help in getting his mind started. Here we find the practical use of a book, especially something like the New Testament or the Imitation of Christ, which helps to stimulate the mind. After that the book can be put aside and the thought can be looked at in itself and then in reference to the one meditating. Some aspect of Our Lord's life is considered, held up to the light and twisted as you would twist a diamond in your fingers as you hold it to the light to see the beautiful colors, "there is green, there is blue, yellow."

Then he asks himself how does this apply to me. I have thought about Our Lord's mercy, let's say to Peter, in forgiving him or to Mary Magdalen. I too am a sinner, I too have offended Him. Hasn't He always taken me back with all of the kindness and love that He showed them? Here come the acts of the will. I tell Him, Lord I am sorry—an act of contrition. Or, I thank You—an act of gratitude. I need You—an act of humility or dependence on God. Or the most perfect act of all, the will at its best—I love You.

As to resolutions, the answer is sometimes yes, sometimes no, but they are not absolutely necessary. In the beginning resolutions will probably be more frequent. I must overcome this fault, this sin, I must show kindness to this my fellow-worker, the one that galls me. I must do an honest day's work for my employer. However, it must be remembered that an act of the will is the end of the prayer and just the very praise of God is something which in itself is even higher than the practical resolution. Prayer is the raising of the mind and heart to God and not to self. That is why in making practical resolutions they must always be made within the framework, within the concept that I will do this because I want to praise and love and serve God better.

Ten minutes each day faithfully adhered to by the lay apostle will gradually develop within him the habit of prayer. He will be able to pray on the bus, walking home from work, in the odd moments of the day. After a time that acts of the mind are lessened and the acts of the will increased. He can find himself in God's presence very quickly now, a simple act of faith in God's presence dwelling within his soul, or in a church an act of faith in the Real Presence of Our Lord on the altar. Then the will comes into play. It should be noted here that the acts of the will, humility, thanksgiving, praise, love, etc., can be and should be repeated frequently, even, if necessary, in the same words. Lovers always repeat themselves.

At this point the lay apostle, in conjunction with his spiritual director, should look out for a period when he can no longer meditate and he can no longer enjoy what we sometimes call a prayer of the affections, which is chiefly concerned with these acts of the will. The ability apparently has gone. The tendency here is to think that something is wrong and nine out of ten people go back to a lower form of prayer. This is where good direction is essential because very frequently this very inability to pray, to meditate, especially after one has been able to meditate for a given time, is a sign that God is taking the soul on to another form of prayer. This time of trial or dryness is a question of God purifying the soul, making it ready to see Him closer at a different and higher level. He is doing in the soul what it would take us years to do by our own unaided efforts. All that the soul can do at this point is to hold on, to make the effort to pray but

55

not to go back to, let's say, formal meditation. This tendency to drift back only holds up the soul in its flight toward God.

Beyond this lies the so-called prayer of quiet and contemplation. Let no one think that these are beyond lay people. God is not limited by states of life. His grace is abundant and, everywhere and to everyone, available. Indeed in our day many more lay people than one realizes have been invited by Him into the realms of passive prayer. We should note in passing how important it is to get direction at this time.

Mental prayer then is really a system of spiritual discipline for the soul and at the same time it is simply the normal development and growth of the soul in love. It tends to make supernatural truths familiar to the mind. These truths and the conviction and action that flow from these truths are extremely important in the formation of the lay apostle. Anyone who wishes to be an ardent lover of God must use this extremely efficacious means of communication.

Why should the lay apostle meditate? There are many reasons. Let's just take two of them. Many years ago a Dominican Prior was giving a talk to his novices on mental prayer. At the end of the talk he said to them: "Brothers, I will guarantee that none of you will ever meditate every day and ever remain in mortal sin. You would have to give up either the meditation or the mortal sinning. You cannot do both. If you try to do both you'll go out of your mind." This was another way of saying what St. Alphonsus Liguori said long before—*mental prayer and mortal sin are incompatible.* In that sense mental prayer is a guarantee of salvation. That is one of the best reasons in the world for meditating.

The other reason is perhaps even more important. Mental prayer will give us conviction about the truths of our faith. Certainly the lay apostle accepts the truths of the faith, and has done so for a long time. But there is a difference between accepting them and being convinced of them. A person who is convinced of the faith is someone who is on fire with it. This is a real apostle. The lay apostle has a message to deliver, a message in the temporal order to his fellow workers and his family and his friends. Unless he is convinced of this message he can hardly deliver it effectively and that is where meditation and mental prayer come in.

LET'S BE PRACTICAL

How does all this idea of mental prayer start? Usually someone, priest or religious, gives the lay apostle a book on mental prayer or meditation. To begin with, the book most likely has been written *by* a priest or religious and *for* priests and religious. It confuses the layman, sometimes frightens him. He gets the idea that this is something very complex, "must be for priests and nuns," he says as he puts the book firmly on the shelf. This is too bad. All one wants to do is to have a lay person think about God and love Him as the result of one's thinking. What is so complex about this? Sometimes the layman also reads about various systems of meditation. Occasionally he gets help here but too often again he is confused. Let us just say at the outset: *If a system of meditation helps you, use it; if it doesn't then forget about it.*

What is the best time to meditate? Well most writers agree that the morning is the better time when the mind is fresh and alert. This is by no means a hard and fast rule especially for lay people. The morning period of prayer is not always possible for the layman. *From a practical point of view an important rule for the lay apostle would seem to be, select a fixed time for each day and then adhere to it faithfully.*

A last word regarding the place of meditation, where should it be conducted? This is important at least for some people. The lay apostle should make some effort to select a quiet spot where distractions are at a minimum. Possibly in his own room (if he has a room) or better still in God's room, a church, where the Eucharistic Presence of Our Lord will no doubt be a positive help for greater devotion.

Let's say it once and for all: *Mental prayer is nothing else except thinking about God with love.* It is not a question of whether one can do it or should do it; it is a question of whether one wants to do it badly enough.

CHAPTER SEVEN

The Lay Apostle's Reading

Whether people realize it or not their reading habits reflect their living habits. It does matter what people read for the simple reason that they think about the things they read and very often end up doing the things they think about. For the fair-minded person this point hardly needs elaboration. Even for that type of person who, in defense of pornographic literature, argues, "It doesn't do anybody any harm," the argument need hardly be pressed. Deep down in his heart he knows he is lying. He knows, almost as well as the next person, that reading and thinking and acting are as closely related as grandmother, mother and daughter—one leads to the other. The murderer who recently went to the chair, insisting that his life of crime began at a newsstand, was putting his finger on the root of the problem, albeit just a little too late for practical resolutions.

If reading habits reflect a person's life, then surely they are important for a lay apostle. Let us first consider what we might call purely spiritual reading which might be said to consist in any form of serious reading that tends to bring the soul closer to God either directly (as for example the Bible, the Imitation of Christ, and other standard spiritual works), or indirectly (such as philosophical or theological works). In these latter, knowledge of the faith is increased and therefore God is attained at least indirectly. This definition would include lives of the saints, Catholic poetry and essays and would not necessarily exclude the serious and purposeful reading of higher-grade Catholic fiction. It would necessarily exclude, however, the reading of a frivolous nature, purely secular study and the so-called "reading for a pastime."

On the other hand there is a form of reading that might be called social reading or possibly sociological or purely intellectual reading. This is very important for the layman. He must be competent within his own field and he must master his own field. If he is a doctor he should know the best writings along his line, a lawyer, the same thing. This type of reading would include most especially the papal encyclicals on the social problems of our day, current papal pronouncements, the writings of men like Cardinal Suhard, the pronouncements of certain episcopates of various countries, for example the pronouncements of our own American Bishops coming out every year, the recent pronouncement of the Canadian Hierarchy on the worker. He should also read weekly or monthly publications on current events such as *Commonweal, America*, a labor paper like *Work* or *The Labor Leader*, a magazine like *Integrity, The Sign, Jubilee* or THE TORCH.

WHY READ?

Reading has many and varied purposes. We have tried to reduce them to three:

Reading supplies the lay apostle with material for thought and therefore with material for meditation. This is important. The frequent assertion, on the part of the lay apostle just beginning to meditate, that, "my mind is a blank," or, "I don't know what to meditate about," find its answer here. It is vitally important that something gets into that mind.

The truths of faith, as elaborated by solid spiritual writers, give the lay apostle the necessary push in the right direction, stimulate a mind that has perhaps become sluggish or inert. St. Teresa of Avila confesses to having been singularly unsuccessful in her meditation for many years unless she had a book to help her. For a lay apostle to go into a period of meditation with a blank mind and to pass a period of time in this state is sheer waste of time, particularly when a good spiritual reading book would start him off in the right direction. We might note here, however, *reading is not meditation and cannot take the place of meditation.* It is a feeder for meditation but these are the thoughts of other people, not our own. Reading is a lot easier than meditation but it can never be a substitute. It is a means, not an end in itself.

Spiritual and social reading disposes ultimately for the love of God since it increases knowledge of God either directly or indirectly. Man cannot possibly love God unless he knows God in some way, whether that knowledge be the knowledge obtained by human reason or the higher form of knowledge enjoyed through faith. Spiritual reading can and does increase this knowledge. The better the reading the better the knowledge and therefore all things being equal the more fervent should be the love.

The lay apostle seriously interested in learning more will readily appreciate the value of spiritual reading. His desire to love God more will drive him to seek to know God better. He seeks not knowledge for knowledge's sake, but knowledge for God's sake. Significantly enough, the lay apostle's spiritual reading should, as he gradually grasps the implications of the apostolate, become more and more discriminating.

Reading on the social doctrine of the Church, papal encyclicals and episcopal pronouncements are vital for the layman. He is trying to love God not in a vacuum but in the modern 20th century where many social institutions are conspiring to make it harder for him to save his soul. He must be aware of these problems. He must see that they have a solution, that sanctity does not consist in entering a church and burying one's head in one's hands while the world is crashing into ruins. This reading then, especially in the modern day, is essential for a good and solid apostolate.

The reading of the lay apostle should inspire him to emulate the people he reads about and the virtues that he finds exemplified in their lives. In a way this is the most important point of all. The lay apostle should be striving to put on Christ, in other words, to become more Christ-like in everything

65

he does. Hence it is essential that he knows what Christ was like and what those other people most closely resembling Christ—the Blessed Mother and the saints—were like. He must come to know not only the historical Christ but the mystical Christ as He is met in the Church today and as he grapples with the problems of our day. This is a reason why, today, so many lay apostolic groups insist that part of their meeting be taken up with the consideration of both "The New Testament" to get the historical Christ and with the Liturgy to make contact with, as we might say, the current Christ.

WHEN?

To agree that spiritual reading is necessary in the life of the lay apostle is a purely speculative conclusion. The next thing is to see that the reading becomes an accomplished fact. Man being what he is, unless he sets for himself a definite time, is inclined to put off things until *mañana*—a process that can become almost a religion with some people. The objection that this is impossible, a set time for reading of a serious nature, that the time is simply not available during the day finds an answer in a very brief but honest examination of conscience. All that a lay apostle has to do is to ask himself how much time do I waste each day or night in light and frivolous reading; how much time do I sit before a television set or a radio; how much time do I give to reading a newspaper. Gradually with discrimination the lay apostle begins to see the sparsity of his intellectual diet and makes time for more substantial fare.

The lay apostle must also learn to utilize odd moments of a day for good reading purposes. So, for example, the book is carried to and from work, to be read on the bus or subway or street car. The before-retiring period is sometimes utilized profitably for solid reading and occasionally part of a lunch period can be used. All of this, like so many other things, is a matter of developing the habit.

WHAT TO READ?

Today, more than ever before, splendid opportunities for short, quick reading are offered, in the form of pamphlets of a devotional, liturgical and intellectual nature. Many of these are extremely well done and worthwhile; many others are a waste of time. The lay apostle must not get the idea that this short quick reading is exhaustive of a given subject nor should he confine himself to this abbreviated form of reading. Sometimes one gets the idea that the pamphlet is the boundary line for the Catholic. This should not be so. The lay apostle especially must learn to figuratively sink his teeth into the meat of Catholic doctrine and literature. Milk is a diet for babies but it would be a tragic mistake to continue that diet once the baby has attained his six-foot majority.

Obviously everything cannot be read. A lay apostle eventually should come to a point of rigid discrimination in reading which we might express in a simple rule: *Read only the best, at your level.* Heading the list at any level there would be the inspired word of God, particularly the New Testament. For some there are the writings of the Fathers and Doctors of the Church, though many could not grasp these. Young workers and young students may find these a bit stiff—or even unavailable. For them a life of a saint well and intelligently written, something like Henri Gheon's "Secrets of the Saints," might be a good starting point. Or especially for the girl, Caryll Houselander's works, "The Reed of God" to name one, or the fine little book "Vocation To Love" by Dorothy Dohen. Going a little heavier, women are usually very pleased with the writings of Father Gerald Vann, O.P., such as "Eve and The Gryphon" or "The Divine

Pity." Needless to say "The Imitation of Christ" is a classic, unique and able to be appreciated by many, though certainly not by all.

Among the devotional literature of our day and other days there is much that is undesirable and time wasting. With the aid of his director the lay apostle should learn to separate the wheat from the chaff. Books today are fairly easy to obtain in public libraries and also in Catholic libraries that are being multiplied in our parishes. At the end of this booklet you will find a selected bibliography, limited of course, but containing some of the outstanding works of our day and other days which we deem important for the use of lay apostles.

CHAPTER EIGHT

Some of the Problems of a Lay Apostle

Like anything worthwhile the task of a lay apostle is not an easy one. The very word "apostle" bespeaks difficulties and the adjective "lay" just adds to it. No apostle in the history of the Church has had an easy time, and consequently, the lay apostle of the 20th century must be prepared for obstacles, even opposition, in the working out of his lay apostolic vocation. This is exactly as it should be. It seems that God tries and purifies man in the accomplishment of anything great. The very presence of trials would seem to be, in many instances, an indication of God's favor rather than of His disfavor. Some of these trials are slight, some grave, but all serve the purpose of convincing the lay apostle that his work, to be truly successful, must be of God and not of man.

The immediate sources of these trials, difficulties, and problems are many and varied. It would be practically impossible to generalize and say that they came from this or that particular source. All that is going to be attempted here is to indicate a few of the common problems of individual apostles and lay apostolic groups in the hope that the airing of these common problems will be of some help in solving other problems, perhaps much more difficult and much more complex.

PROBLEMS ORIGINATING WITH THE LAY APOSTLE

Of all the problems that originate in the soul of the lay apostle perhaps the most common and the most dangerous is the one of pride. Here is a lay person suddenly thrown into the apostolate of the Catholic Church, in a greater or limited manner, whatever the case might be. He is untrained, inexperienced, and yet on fire to work for the good of God and the salvation of neighbor. He has a new *status*, an important one; he has, as it were, become over night a hunter of souls, a task that has been the prerogative of saints, bishops, priests, and scholars throughout the centuries. Perhaps he is highly respected, particularly by those closest to him. It is precisely here that pride enters, or may enter. St. Augustine points out wisely in his Rule: "Pride enters even into good works to destroy them." There is a danger that the lay apostle might begin concentrating on what *he* is doing in the apostolate *rather than on what Christ is doing through him*. Basically it is a misunderstanding of the action of divine grace. "Without Me you can do nothing." "I can do all things in Him who strengthens me."

The lay apostle must realize to the very depths of his soul that his task is to spread Christ and not himself. All of which is quite easy to say but much harder to accomplish. The failure to come to this realization, to put it into practice, argues fundamentally a lack of humility. In the early stages of the lay apostle's life this is often the case and is too frequently a cause of discouragement, failure and also, let it be said, the cause of many defections from the lay apostolic vocation.

Another problem one must avoid is the notion that there is any such thing as mass produced or assembly-line formation. There is no short cut here. The apostolate of Christ is essentially a matter of grace both for the apostolate and for the apostle. One can be a "go getter" only insofar as he goes to Christ and gets from Christ what ultimately he is to give to others.

Still another problem that the lay apostle creates for himself (again possibly through pride) is opposition from other lay apostles and other lay apostolic groups. The old question of jealousy or envy. Untold damage has been done by overly zealous and unenlightened lay apostles who take it upon themselves to label other groups as ineffective and inadequate, always, of course, in comparison with the particular group or organization to which they happen to belong. There should be an end to this and every group should firmly stamp this sort of thing out of existence. A spirit of competition, or worse still, opposition is directly contrary to the mind of the Church as expressed in the unmistakable writings of the last few Vicars of Christ on earth. The word is *cooperation*.

FAMILY PROBLEMS

Scripture says that a man's enemies are those of his own household. Perhaps this throws some light on the fact (even though it doesn't necessarily explain it) that the lay apostle very frequently meets his strongest opposition in his own household. The root of the problem is usually misinformation or ignorance. It is very common for young girls especially to run up against tremendous opposition from parents.

In all justice it must be remembered that the lay apostolate was practically unheard of in our parents' day and so, naturally enough, they find it difficult to reconcile the ideas and actions of their sons and daughters with those of their own day. Archbishop Charbonneau of Montreal in his "Pastoral Letter on Catholic Action" took note of this strange phenomenon. "Too many parents," the Archbishop wrote, "unfortunately, still hinder the onward march of Catholic Action by creating for them difficulties which are truly inexplicable."

This problem can become at times most serious. The lay apostle must recognize the parental opposition for what it is, namely misinformation, a lack of understanding of the true nature of the lay apostolate, and he, the lay apostle, must therefore take prudent measures to remedy such a situation. Sometimes simple explanations will be accepted and understood. It is especially well for lay apostles to make their parents feel they are a part of their thinking. Wherever possible groups should include certain activities for parents to initiate them into ideas of the apostolate and ideas that their children bring home.

Sometimes prudence would dictate that any instruction of parents by children be given obliquely and indirectly. One practical way is to bring other lay apostles to the home where, in the give and take of social contact, and by their very presence and example, these other lay apostles may be able to dispel any parental fear, opposition or ignorance. G. K. Chesterton used to believe very much in the psychology of ironing out difficulties and of carrying on fruitful conversation over a dinner table. At least it is worth a try.

In the case of young girls, sometimes it almost seems as though the parents fear that entanglement in the lay apostolate will present a real threat to the possibility of a future, happy and successful marriage for their daughters. To get very practical about this problem, it should be noted the lay apostolate normally should help toward a happy marriage rather than hinder. Monsignor Joseph Cardijn, after thirty years of experiment and after much success in Belgium, has been quoted as saying that the greatest result of his work so far has been the thousands and thousands of happy Christian families that his form of the lay apostolate has helped establish. God knows there are enough unhappy marriages in our day. Parents should be consoled and should understand that marriage is not a matter of getting the first one that comes along but of getting the best one that comes along and of building from that point on.

From the newly married lay apostle's point of view it should be noted in passing that his or her apostolate does not end with marriage; it just changes. There is a family apostolate, in the United States known as the Christian Family Movement, which is just as important as the one they left behind. Young married couples who have been trained as true lay apostles are the hope of the Church in restoring Christ to those family circles from which He has been so thoroughly and so shamefully excluded. The Christian Family Movement and young Christian married couples have a staggering task awaiting them.

RETREATS AND DAYS OF RECOLLECTION AS A PARTIAL ANSWER

This is not the sole function of a retreat or a day of recollection by any means—to help solve problems. We have seen that retreats and days of recollection are a necessary part of the lay apostle's plan of life. They can, however, help very much to bring individuals and groups "back on the beam," to help the group examine its status, to help the lay apostle evaluate his failures and his success. And of course they have the function of planning for the future.

Almost all groups make some provision for a yearly three-day closed retreat for lay apostles and frequently for quarterly days of recollection or even monthly days of recollection. Some groups have what they call study days, days of intensive examination of parts of their program, days wherein their plans are appraised and perfected. All this is to the good. It is also very heartening to see the tremendous growth of the retreat movement in the United States and to see the valiant efforts that are being made to serve the needs of lay apostles by what might be called specialized retreats, retreats for young workers, for young business women, family retreats wherein husband and wife make a retreat together (a marvelous idea that has the practical difficulty of finding facilities for married couples and baby-sitters for the children). Many retreat houses, colleges and institutions have been most generous in making their facilities available for the use of lay apostolic groups. This is, of course, only as it should be. The late Pontiff, Pius XI, used to frequently admonish one of the great retreat orders of the Church that they should always open their doors to lay apostles.

CHAPTER NINE

Leisure Time

When Pope Pius X, that enlightened and blessed Pontiff, asked and included in his motto the idea that all things be restored in Christ, he meant just that. He said *Omnia*, "all things." He meant all things. He wanted Christ brought back into every phase of human life, the home, family life, factory, the office, the crafts, the arts, even into that lighter phase of man's life known as his leisure time and that more specific phase known as his recreation. The general public, even the ordinary Catholic, missed Pius X's point completely, if indeed they were aware that he had made a point. Secularism, at that time as today, was in their eyes and had sold people the idea that God and religion should occupy a nice little corner of man's life and that He should be kept there. Religion, they said in effect, is fine on Sundays but on Monday morning "business is business," and on Saturday night "pleasure is king."

Happily, however, there were those who got the point and who began, slowly at first, to attempt restoring Christ to His rightful place. Organized and specialized Catholic Action groups as well as innumerable other forms of the lay apostolate began restoring Christ to His rightful place in the affairs of men. Countries like Belgium, Holland, France, responded magnificently; others were slower in grasping the idea. But practically all have come to see in greater or lesser degree what the saintly Pope Pius X had in mind.

It is not at all strange that one of the first problems attacked by many of these groups was the use of man's leisure time and the obvious problem of modern recreation. After all this was plainly a field from which Christ had generally been excluded.

Leisure is coming to play a more important part in man's life. Mr. Hilaire Belloc used to write about the Servile State. We are now beginning to get a little concerned at least in some parts of the world with the "Leisure State." In the United States the 40-hour week is very common. More and more one is finding a 35-hour week. How is the resulting free time going to be used?

It is probably true that because of modern industrialism recreation and leisure time are more needed today than ever before. Pope Leo XIII in his classic, *Rerum Novarum*, seems to indicate this in more than one place. He enunciated what might be called a general rule in this same encyclical when he said: "As a general principle it may be laid down, that a workman ought to have leisure and rest in proportion to the wear and tear of his strength . . ." Naturally the Pontiff didn't say how much a part recreation should play in a man's life, what he should do with his leisure time, what types of activities should be employed at this time. These are different questions entirely and can best be worked out by the people involved—the laity.

At the outset we might distinguish leisure time from recreation. Leisure time is the broader term and indeed includes recreation. For example, leisure time might be spent not only in playing a basketball game but it might be spent in study or prayer or simply resting. Recreation, on the other hand, means just what the word says, to recreate, to create anew. St. Thomas saw recreation as a Christian virtue *eutrapelia*, and he analyzed recreation as properly consisting in the idea of resting after work in some manner that would relieve the tensions of mind or body and of preparing for more work by way of the recreation. All work and no play not only makes Jack a dull boy; eventually it may kill him. At the same time, work and the wrong kind of play makes Jack a bad boy, or a very tiresome one. In other words, the moderation in recreation must fall not only on the fact of recreation but also on its manner and circumstance. Throwing and running and kicking are generally considered ordinary forms of recreation, but one must also be concerned with what one throws, why one runs, and who or what on kicks—and why.

The lay apostle must be, as it were, jealous of his leisure time. It is not his. It belongs to Christ. Therefore it must be used for Christ. Certainly he needs leisure, positively he needs recreation, the important thing is to get it and to get it in proportion. One of the bigger problems of his life and of every layman's life today is involved in the field of recreation where so much of it is of a kind that either distracts or impairs one's personality. For that reason many of the things we have to say in this chapter will touch more properly on recreation rather than leisure. It should be noted too that a dedicated lay apostle ordinarily does not have too much difficulty in this matter of either leisure or recreation. The apostolate itself gives him a field of activity that sometimes might be too absorbing or too demanding. The various forms of the apostolate frequently provide recreational facilities, outings, parties, socials, and so forth. However, not only does the lay apostle have the problem of leisure and recreation in his own life, he must also consider this as a problem in the life of his fellowman.

TV AND THE MOVIES

With the advent of television and with the universal dissemination of the motion picture many problems have come up in regard to these two modes of recreation. Pope Pius XI in his encyclical letter on Improper Motion Pictures pointed out the fact that this form of communication, the motion picture, has achieved "a position of universal importance among modern means of diversion . . . the most popular form of diversion which is offered for the leisure moments, not only of the rich, but all the masses of society." As recently as January 2, 1954, Pope Pius XII passed devastating judgment on motion pictures when he stigmatized them as "the foremost corrupter of youth."

The Pontiff also feared the spread of the corruption when we shall have the motion picture in every living room by way of the TV set. This is the greatest educational device, for good or for bad, that the world has ever known. As that great pioneer of the lay apostolate, Monsignor Joseph Cardijn, said on first looking at a TV program: "This changes everything."

Education for good or for bad, recreation, diversion or perversion. Take your pick. A very great problem today is the tendency to see television or the movies as an escape, a tendency to sit before the screen and let everything pass before the eyes sometimes without admitting it to the mind, sometimes soaking it all in. There has to be moderation here and discrimination and one must learn to pick and choose here as in everything else. The lay apostle must not be willing to see his Christian principles degraded, no more than he should check them at the box office on entering a movie. He cannot, if he is a thinking apostle, sit there side by side with his non-thinking Catholic friend wringing his (or her) handkerchief, hoping that somehow or another the handsome husband will get rid of his not-so-attractive wife and marry his oh-so-attractive secretary. The fact that this is often what happens both in movies and before the TV screen and that everyone, including the Catholics, go home happy about the whole affair doesn't make it any the less ridiculous. This is not recreation, it is desecration, particularly of the mind whereby a rational Catholic lets his mind, his intelligence be insulted by a lot of nonsense that is contrary to all that Christ taught. The lay apostle must learn to discriminate on programs and movies to make sure that he is getting only the best and also, let it be said, that he is getting it in proper doses and not being overfed Just as one is very careful with the food that one takes into the body so one should also be more especially careful with the food that feeds the mind and the soul.

TV and motion pictures are just one problem. There are many others, for example, reading, modern dancing, radio, modern music. What about these? What, for example, the lay apostle must ask himself, what does he think of certain forms of modern music? What about that modern jungle music that so many people inflict upon themselves and others. Is it, can it be recreational in any sense of the word or does it dissipate? And what about certain types of dancing? Is this good or dangerous or indifferent? In his encyclical *Ubi Arcano*, the late Pope Pius XI as far back as 1922 noted: "we lament, too, the destruction of purity among women and young girls as evidenced by the increasing immodesty

87

of their dress and conversation and by their participation in shameful dances . . ."

Occasionally we of the 20th century are highly amused, in our smug, provincial way, as we attend a newsreel and see the queer antics displayed by certain jungle dancers from the Zulu Islands or Timbuktu. On the other hand the Zulu Islanders and the Timbuktu-ers, in their provincial way, would probably be amused beyond words at the indescribable gyrations of their civilized brethren and sisters as expressed in some forms of the modern dance.

ACTIVITY VERSUS PASSIVITY

Recreation today has become more and more passive in nature. This is obviously the case in the things we have discussed—television, the movies. As a matter of fact one cannot help but notice that one of the more popular forms of television programs that seem to get good ratings are those that involve quizzes where the spectator as well as the participants are challenged to think. Passivity is obviously the case in spectator sports where thousands of workers, in need of activity themselves, sit and watch highly trained, and even more highly paid, athletes function on a football gridiron, a baseball diamond, a tennis court or a boxing ring. These things at best are lopsidedly passive from the spectator's point of view.

Recreation implies more than this. Recreation is not rest. Rest can be obtained by sleeping, and sleeping can hardly be considered recreation (though, as we mentioned, it could be part of leisure time) except by a decided minority of devotees. Recreation more properly implies change and diversion. It means that a man should use his faculties and especially those faculties that, in the immediate past, have been dormant and inactive. A professional athlete, for example, should, and probably often does, seek his recreation not in athletics but in reading or study where he exercises his mind. The scholar on the other hand might well enjoy his recreation in some bodily form of activity.

As a result of many factors in present day life the lay apostle discovers that many one-time popular and active forms of recreation have literally become *passé*. Walking, for example, a decidedly active function, has become somewhat of a lost art. Because of the constant and habitual use of other forms of locomotion one of man's most prized faculties has been gradually falling into desuetude. The art of conversation is another thing at issue. This has deteriorated to such an extent that many times conversation today can hardly be termed rational, much less recreational, except by the most charitable. What can be said about a ceaseless discussion on fingernail polish, a boring repetition of moron jokes or the thousand-and-one inanities that go by the name and make up modern gossip. Passive forms of recreation have stultified thinking and when people no longer think they cease to converse or at least to converse in a way that one could call serious or recreational.

This loss of the power of thinking is serious. Constant contact with inferior minds has brought about a mental paralysis. One almost feels like the dog shown in the cartoon with the master saying "Speak," and the animal answering "What will I say?"

SUGGESTIONS

All of this and much more must be investigated in order that Christ find His rightful place in man's social and sociable life. Lay apostolic groups in particular should make careful studies of the recreational habits of their members and friends in order to improve the situation. As in everything else, any reform must start with the individual. People are not going to like being told that the recreation they prize so dearly is in reality a decidedly inferior thing or possibly no recreation at all. Man is a creature of habit and he gets enamored of some decidedly strange forms of diversion by reason of this very fact. People are used to it; therefore they do it. Consequently a lay apostle to be effective must first have found the answer to the problems of his own recreational life and his own leisure time before he can validly ask a hearing from other. Above all the negative approach should be avoided here. People do not like to have a thing taken away unless something better is put in its place. It is up to the lay apostle to be ready with better ideas, he must arrange, organize, create things that surpass the things that people are doing. He and his fellow apostles must offer better shows, possibly amateur dramatics, in the place of the ever-powerful, yet Christless, movies and TV. This of course has the added advantage that it is an active form of recreation and gives many people opportunities to express themselves.

Even the things that people have been doing can be organized so that they are better dances, better shows, better picnics, better discussion groups. Speaking of dancing, some good folk-dancing of a wholesome and highly recreational nature can often supplant some of the questionable modern forms of dancing. This has another advantage in that it brings about a better group participation, the whole family, the whole parish, the whole club, dances together.

Many of these ideas will meet opposition, in certain quarters they will be positively disapproved. However, disapproval does not mean a destruction of the idea. Because certain people cannot (or will not) see a point, the point remains unless disproven by solid and reasonable argument.

People today must also be brought into contact with finer minds than their own. This is another way of saying they should do some reading. The lay apostle, by his own example, could try a diet of Chesterton, Trese and Sheed instead of Dick Tracy and Li'l Abner. It might be a fine thing if families would begin shutting off their television sets after listening to a good educational program and carry the discussion a bit further themselves. We have to create an atmosphere wherein people realize that they have minds and wherein they'll be anxious to use them, that they have ideas that can and should be expressed even though the ideas do not come out in the effortless smooth-flowing talk of a high-salaried commentator or news analyst. The lay apostle can urge home entertainment with games, cards, songfests, in place of the stupid night-clubs with their professional entertainers, high prices and bored clientele. Actually the possibilities are almost endless. We do need, however, people with ideas and with courage.

Speaking of courage in one sense this is the crux of this question. It takes courage to be different today. Regardless of the fact that the lay apostle or lay apostolic groups may seem to be knocking their collective heads against a wall, they cannot give up. The leisure time of a human being does matter. Souls are being lost here just as they are being lost at work. Christ must be included here, He must be returned to the leisure and the recreational time of every soul that He created. All things must be restored to Him, in Him and for Him. It is not an easy task but that fact alone does not render it any way the less important.

CHAPTER TEN

Third Orders

It might be well here to say just a word about the lay apostle and the Third Orders of the Church. One of the biggest problems that the lay apostle inevitably faces is that of coordinating his interior spiritual life with his active apostolate. Human nature being what it is, there is, too often, the tendency to stress the one to the neglect of the other. As a consequence sometimes the would-be lay apostle is found dashing about madly doing things for others, while blithely forgetting, or ignoring entirely, the indisputable fact that one cannot give what one does not have. On the other hand, we sometimes come across the other type, the one who literally spends all his life in personal formation to the complete neglect of the apostolate. This one is always "getting ready," but no one (not even him-himself) knows what for, or when. Either extreme is fatal.

The first type, the activist, may turn out to be a first class humanitarian, a well-intentioned philanthropist, or he may simple be a victim of glands. By no stretch of the imagination can he be called an apostle, for the simple reason that he has no message to deliver. The second type may be, ostensibly, a very holy person, but as far as the apostolate is concerned he is simply "not ready" and probably never will be ready. After all, if one must wait for sanctity before acting when will anyone act, who will say "go," how did all the people who are acting get started?

The problem for the lay apostle then is to coordinate the interior and the active. This is not exactly a problem of separation but of timing. One complements the other. According to the Angelic Doctor, St. Thomas, contemplation prepares for action and action prepares for contemplation. *However, the effective action of a lay apostle is proportioned to his spiritual formation.* The conclusion from this fact is obvious. The faster the spiritual formation the deeper, the more integrated, the more effective will be his apostolate in life. We must also understand that, as we mentioned before, there is such a thing as formation through action and that psychologically this is decidedly important. However, this is just one means of formation, it is not the only one.

The Sacramental Life of the Church, the Liturgy, private and liturgical prayer, mortification, meditation, contemplation are vast storehouses of grace that the lay apostle must learn to draw upon regularly. We have touched upon most of these. There remains one special means that has not been treated and that is a part that a Third Order can play in the life of a lay apostle. This is not a *sine qua non*, one does not have to belong to a Third Order to be an effective lay apostle. However, many lay apostles have recognized the important part that a Third Order can play in their lives. *De facto* vast numbers among the lay apostolate belong to some approved Third Order. The Church has made Third Orders available for this reason, as a help and a safeguard for the generous laity.

WHAT IS A THIRD ORDER?

A Third Order is actually a group or association of lay people who, while living in the world, share, nevertheless, in the spiritual life of a religious Order to which they belong and under whose direction they are. The term "Third Order" is easily explained. In the Dominican Order, for example, the priests and lay brothers belong to the First Order, the strictly cloistered nuns belong to the Second Order and the Third Order has two branches. There is the Third Order Regular (the sister) and the Third Order Secular (lay people and secular priests—for secular priests may belong to the Third Order). The term "Third Order" has become canonized to designate people living in the world but attached to a religious Order.

The Third Order is a real part of the whole Order. The members of the Third Order share in the rights and privileges of the Order itself, insofar as their state allows. Tertiaries are expected to wear some inconspicuous symbol of the Order which takes the place of the habit. Usually this consists of a small scapular, the color of the habit and is worn under the clothes. Formerly Tertiaries wore the full habit even while living in the world, a fact that accounts for certain Tertiary saints, such as Catherine of Siena, being mistaken for nuns. A Third Order is not a Confraternity nor a Pious Association. The chief purpose of a Confraternity is the promotion of public worship, while a Pious Union has for its purpose the exercise of some particular works of piety and charity. *A Third Order, on the other hand, is a way of life and its members are committed, although not under vow, to strive for perfection.* Canon Law gives precedence to the Third Order over all other lay associations in the Church.

Every Third Order has a Papally approved Rule outlining the obligations, privileges, end, means and spirit, etc., of the particular Order. These Rules, of course, differ according to the spirit of the various Orders, but all generally seek to bring the spirit of the cloister into the world. None of these rules binds the Tertiary under pain of sin. Membership in a Third Order is always preceded by a period of novitiate and, in some cases, by a period of postulancy.

Prayer, of course, is featured in the Third Order Rules. Liturgical, or quasi-liturgical prayer, is usually enjoined. Tertiaries very often recite daily one of the Little Offices of the Church, which vary in length and are actually abbreviations of the Divine Office. All Third Orders allow for the substitution of the Rosary or some other shorter prayers for Tertiaries who are unable to fulfill the obligation of the Little Office. There are usually also certain pious practices enjoined, such as fasting on stated days and prayers for the dead. Meetings are held, ordinarily once a month, and are carried out under the direction of a priest of the Order.

Today there are eight Third Orders in the Church; the Augustinians, Carmelites, Dominicans, Franciscans, Minims (not in this country), Premonstratensians, Servites and Trinitarians. The Benedictines have Oblates who are not Tertiaries but roughly correspond to them. It has been estimated that there are about 200,000 Tertiaries in the United States. One hundred twenty-five thousand of these are Franciscans, who also have, by far, the largest group in the entire world. Many Third Orders are organized into Fraternities or Chapters while some, such as the Dominicans, for example, also make provision for private Tertiaries who, for some reason or another, cannot join a particular Fraternity. The Franciscan and possibly some of the other Orders take members at fourteen; the Dominicans will not receive anyone until the completion of the eighteenth year, although, for a good reason, dispensation allows admittance at seventeen. The Dominican Third Order in this country is probably second to the Franciscan in number of members.

THE THIRD ORDER OF ST. DOMINIC

Like every other Third Order, the Dominican Third Order follows the general spirit of the First Order. The motto that expresses the spirit of the Dominican Order is "to contemplate and to give to others the fruits of our contemplation." The end or goal of the Third Order is the perfection of its members, which is brought about, as the Rule notes "by the practice of a more perfect Christian life and the promotion of the salvation of souls in a way that is suitable to the state of the faithful living in the world." (No. 2). The means for obtaining this end, over and above the precepts and duties of one's state in life, are the observance of the Rule, continual prayer and, as far as possible, liturgical prayer, penance, apostolic and charitable works for the Faith and the Church according to one's condition and particular state in life (No. 3).

The end and means of the Third Order are designed to bear out the general ideal and idea of the Order. The word *Veritas*, "Truth," is to be found emblazoned on the shield of the Dominican Order. Just as the Franciscan Order seeks to attain its end by stressing poverty and charity, so also does the Dominican Order attain its end by seeking Truth.

The Dominican Tertiary, like the Dominican First Order member, must always accentuate truth. That is why the Rule says that Tertiaries should be ardent defenders of the rights of the Church and the Pope in all things and at all times.

They should also, the Rule says, help in Apostolic works, particularly those of the Order (No. 41).

Truth belongs to all and not to just the few. He who has the truth necessarily has the obligation of imparting it to others. Hence a Dominican Tertiary should be a leader in such matters as study, reading, the examination of Papal Encyclicals, the formation of study clubs, discussion groups and, especially in this country, the preparation of trained and expert teachers for the Confraternity of Christian Doctrine. By rule he is obliged to be a willing assistant to the parish priest both in pious works and in imparting religious instruction to the young (No. 43). A Dominican Tertiary must also, under the direction of the superior, devote himself to works of charity and mercy (No. 42).

To view the Dominican Third Order, as many do, as a school of individual perfection and nothing more, is a fatal yet common mistake. It is a school of perfection but it is also apostolic, and to miss this point is to miss the entire genius of St. Dominic who was an apostle to his fingertips. The fact that individual Tertiaries and even individual Fraternities may be missing this point argues not against Tertiary Life but against the non-observance of Tertiary Life and Rule.

THIRD ORDERS AND THE LAY APOSTOLATE

The Third Orders of the Church have been and can be a great help in the development of lay apostles and the lay apostolate itself. A lay apostle obviously needs discipline and order in his life. Third Order Rules are designed for this very purpose. Moreover they are, and this should never be forgotten, *Papally approved Rules*, having behind them hundreds of years of experience, Rules that have produced what they guarantee to produce when followed faithfully—*lay sanctity*.

A great obstacle in the way of the lay apostle is the so-called "heresy of good works," the real danger of an activism that would send the lay apostle dashing out to do things for others, forgetting the obvious fact that one cannot give what one does not have to give. The lay apostle, as Dom Chautard points out, can and often does make the fatal mistake of looking for success in his own personal activity, his talents, his clever organization. Grace is disregarded, prayer neglected, sometimes pride enters in. These things happen, make no mistake. To take the attitude that such a state is impossible in the life of a lay apostle is to ignore the true nature of man. A Third Order Rule of life is a tremendous help at this point. One might also formulate an axiom: *The lay apostle who is living his life according to the Rule of a Third*

Order cannot possibly fall into the heresy of good works. The Rule of life will not allow this. As long as he follows the Rule he is safe. Not only that, but his active life should be the more fruitful in proportion to his adherence to the Rule. His apostolate, on the other hand, must, of necessity, be genuine, particularly where the Third Order Rule calls for the active apostolate as in the case of certain Orders such as the Carmelites, Franciscans, Dominicans.

The charge sometimes made that a Third Order develops sanctity but not an apostolic saint arises from a strange concept of sanctity and an even stranger concept of apostolicity. Just a cursory glance at a few Tertiary saints would dispel this illusion. The wool dyer's daughter Catherine of Siena, Elizabeth of Hungary a Queen, the accomplished Thomas More of England, the fragile Rose of Lima, and in our own day, the reformed alcoholic Matt Talbot, all managed in their own way to accomplish quite a lot of apostolic work while following a Third Order Rule of life.

The many priests engaged in forming lay apostles are looking for authentic agencies of formation. Let it be said at the outset that the priest himself is a great agency. However, the Church has through her Third Orders given an authentic agency to them. We have the demand; the Third Orders have at least part of the supply.

It would be well, therefore, for chaplains of Catholic Action, and other lay apostolic groups, to look into the possibilities of Third Order help along this line. The lay apostle himself should seriously investigate the Third Orders since they are designed by the Church to meet one of his most pressing needs. All Third Orders are not alike. Each strikes a distinct note that is in harmony with the whole but which, at the same time, is especially attuned to the spirit of the Religious Order to which it is attached. One sounds *Pax*, another *Caritas*, another *Gloria Dei*. The Dominicans sound *Veritas*, claiming that they fulfill their task in seeking and in propagating *Truth*. As Saint Paul so beautifully says: "Now there are varieties of gifts but the same spirit; and there are varieties of ministries, but the same Lord; and there are varieties of workers, but the same God who works all things in all."

CHAPTER ELEVEN

The Young Christian Workers— a Form of the Lay Apostolate

At this point we might look at a particular form of the lay apostolate to see how it operates, particularly as to its ideas and its methods. We have chosen the Young Christian Worker Movement, that dynamic Movement founded back in 1912 by a parish priest, Canon Joseph Cardijn, and approved by the Holy See in 1925. We have selected the Young Christian Workers not because they are necessarily the best or the most successful form of the lay apostolate, but because their methods are most widely known and used and also because this Movement, sometimes referred to as the Jocist, *Jeunesse Ouvriere Chretienne*, Young Christian Workers, has received from its very inception the wholehearted approval of both Pope Pius XI and more recently Pope Pius XII. The former Pontiff said: "We give this Movement as an example to Catholic Action." Pope Pius XII has spoken of the astounding results of "a Movement on which Providence seems to have set its seal."

Only last November, 1953, in a special audience with Monsignor Cardijn, His Holiness is quoted as having said: "I bless the Young Christian Workers and I desire its extension to the working youth of the whole world." We have also selected this particular Movement because so many other forms of the lay apostolate, practically all of the specialized Catholic Action Movements, have used and adapted the Young Christian Worker methods and technique.

THE SO-CALLED "CELL" TECHNIQUE

When Canon Cardijn first met His Holiness Pope Pius XI, he did so under rather peculiar circumstances. Merely by accident the young Fr. Cardijn walked into a room and found himself in the presence of our Holy Father. Abashed and nervous, he said the first thing that came to his mind: "Holy Father, I want to give my life for the masses of the people."

The one sentence caught the ear and the imagination of Pius XI, and he told the young parish priest that all the time people were coming to him with plans and with schemes and that they always involved an elite group of people. "You are the first one," he said, "that has come to me to speak about the masses of the people." From that time forward his Holiness received Joseph Cardijn every single year of his life, and it was particularly and especially this idea of reaching the ordinary working class people that captivated the mind and the imagination of the great Pope of Catholic Action.

The Young Christian Worker Movement is a mass Movement. By that is meant that they aim at reaching all young workers, influencing all parts of life, educating, representing and serving the young workers of the world in every phase of their life whether it be social, educational, recreational, economic, moral, spiritual. They do this by a very simple method which is sometimes called the "cell technique." The idea is that the dynamic group today must be a small group, a group made up of between six and eight young workers between the ages of approximately sixteen and twenty-eight. This group is a group that is trained and formed through their own study methods and through the help of a chaplain; but they are trained and formed to turn not in, but out to others, to their fellow-workers, to the boy and girl next to them in the shop or the factory or the office. They are trained to turn out with the spirit of love and conquest toward the members of their natural environment. In this way each member of that little group of six or eight begins to develop what is sometimes referred to as "teams" or "action groups," other fellows and girls, friends of theirs, acquaintances, who meet with them fairly regularly and either formally or informally discuss the problems of the working life, the home life, the family life, the recreational life that they have, and who plan also, (and this is extremely important) on doing something about it. The group is always turned out, it is an apostolic group. This spirit of conquest ("we need not fear the revolution, we are the revolution"), channels its way down into the teams or action groups and out toward a larger group of workers that might be called the "mass."

A fellow or girl may or may not have any interest in the Church, in an apostolate, or, for that matter, in anything. These too must be reached. These are workers with immortal souls, with an innate and a marvelous dignity, they are sons and daughters of God living His divine Life whether they know it or not. Christ died for each one of them. Christ would have died for any one of them if that one were the only person in the world. The Young Christian Workers are trained and schooled in the concept that everyone is important, that Christ is living or might be living in every young worker in the world. The central group of six or eight "leaders," as they are sometimes called, and the team or action group usually meet weekly. The larger group, their friends and so-called "contacts" ordinarily meet monthly.

THE MEETING

Each section of the YCW consisting of the leader's group, the action group and the general membership has a chaplain. He is the representative of the Church, the guarantee of the orthodoxy of the group, the one most responsible for the formation of the members, but not, and this is important, the leader of the group. The leader of the group is a lay person, a young worker, for this is a *lay movement*.

Before each meeting, which is usually held weekly, the chaplain prepares the meeting with the leader, he goes over it point by point, not telling the leader how to conduct the meeting but drawing from him, his, the lay person's, ideas. This too is important. Lay leadership and lay initiative must be developed and encouraged. The priest is a sort of guide, a safety valve sometimes, possibly a court of last appeal, but he is not the leader of the group nor does he lead the weekly meeting. The problems discussed are the problems of daily life—the problems of a worker at his bench, a boy and his family and a girl and her fiancé. Here is where lay competence pays off and the priest-chaplain of a YCW group is the first one to see the extreme importance of developing the lay character of the apostolate.

The meeting of a Young Christian Worker group lasts ordinarily about an hour and a half and follows a fairly general pattern. It opens with a prayer, there is then the check-up on action and review of influence at which is determined how the actions of the week previous have been carried out and what influence is being worked out by the group on their environment. Next there comes the Gospel inquiry wherein there is a short discussion on some part of Our lord's life and an application of this to the worker's daily life. There then takes place the important part of the meeting, the social inquiry, wherein the program for the month is discussed and action taken on it each week by each member. Finally, some point of the Liturgy, the Mass, or the Sacraments gets a ten-minute discussion and the meeting ends with prayer.

The prayer that opens the meeting is usually the beautiful Young Christian Worker prayer which goes as follows:

'Lord Jesus, I offer Thee this day all my works, my hopes and struggles, my joys and sorrows. Grant me and all my fellow workers the grace to think like Thee, to work with Thee and to live in Thee. Make me able to love Thee with all my heart and serve Thee with all my strength. Thy kingdom come in all our factories, workshops, offices, schools, and in all our homes. May those of us who may be in danger of sin remain in Thy grace, and may those who have died on labor's field of honor rest in peace.' 'Sacred Heart of Jesus, bless the Young Christian Workers; Sacred Heart of Jesus, Thy kingdom come through the Young Christian Workers.'

THE INQUIRY

It is not enough, however, to try and reach the masses of workers. It is a question of once you reach them, what are you going to give them and how do you know what to give them? This is where the famous inquiry technique of the Young Christian Workers comes in. The inquiry is one of the great tools used by this Movement whereby their plan of action is studied and carried out. The inquiry is an educational device for arriving at prudent action. Canon Cardijn lifted it bodily from St. Thomas Aquinas. In the *Summa Theologica* (IIa., IIae., q.51,a 1-4), St. Thomas asked what are the three steps in arriving at a prudent action, his answer was Counsel, Judgment and Command. The great pioneer of the lay apostolate, Canon Cardijn, simply changed and simplified these expressions to "See, Judge, Act." So popular has this technique become that it is employed by almost all of the specialized Catholic Action groups in the world today as well as by innumerable other groups of lay apostles.

The first thing to note is the naturalness of this technique—one sees, judges and acts before one does anything that makes any sense. To cross a New York street one must prudently see the traffic light, what is its color, how long has it been green, how wide is the street? Then one must judge, can I make it, will that cab that is catapulting down the street stop for me, can I get to the other side before the light turns red and I find myself inundated on both sides in the middle of the street, surrounded by monstrous taxi cabs? Then action, I cross the street. If my observation and my judgment have been correct I arrive on the other side. This method is used with all the programs of the Young Christian Workers. A large program, such as the worker and his work, is broken down to a week-by-week small portion of this program and an action is decided upon. We have penned here a typical inquiry taken from a YCW program published at the YCW Headquarters, 638 West Deming Place, Chicago, Illinois.

SOCIAL INQUIRY: JOB SECURITY

Observe:

1. How many young workers do you know who work in places where workers are constantly being fired?
2. Of the workers you know, how many have lately expressed the fear of being laid off? Of jobs being harder to get?
3. Has this changed their attitude toward their present job in any way? Give facts which show this.

Judge:

1. What are the effects of job insecurity on the young worker—now? In the future?

2. What would be the young worker's greatest safeguard against exploitation? Explain.
3. Will this problem be solved if young workers themselves don't feel their responsibility? Why?
4. Why must *we* educate them in this?

Act:

1. Can we make some of our fellow workers aware of the cases where layoffs and firing are a danger and awaken them to their responsibility in the matter?
2. What can we do about places of work where irresponsible firing is practiced—through the union if it exists, through other representative action? How will we go about it?

Secondly, and this is one of the most telling aspects of the inquiry, it begins where people, ordinary people, begin. Canon Cardijn discovered many years ago in dealing with the working class people that they work, that they learn things, from the practical back to the speculative. In other words, that working class people ordinarily learn *a posteriori*, that they begin with their problems and that you can then take them back to the principles. Unlike himself as a priest who was trained *a priori*, the young workers that Canon Cardijn dealt with were concerned and would talk about their wages, their families, their courtship, their economic and social and moral problems. These people were factual. From that point they could be encouraged to make a judgment as to whether these things were good or bad, and beyond that something could be done about changing the bad to the good or improving the good.

The inquiry method in the hands of the YCW has become a tremendous educational device. This is education for the masses, education for people who may or may not read books, for people who, for the most part, do not have time to take out to go to schools and colleges and universities. Yet make no mistake about this, these people over a long period of time are educated. What is more they are educated in life, they know how to apply the things they have learned for the simple reason that they apply them every day in every circumstance of their life. Through this device young workers come to realize they have a Divine destiny, that Christ died for them and for every other one of their fellow workers. They come to understand the Incarnation, the Mass, the Redemption. They live the doctrine of the

Mystical Body, applying it *where they are* and in ways that only their own ingeniousness can prompt them to take.

The third great accomplishment of the inquiry method is that it does end in action, not any action, but prudent action. This is no matter of a study club or a discussion group that ends in sterile speculation. Each week every one of the members is expected to take definite action in his environment. This worker is new, he feels unaccepted. I'll invite him out to lunch. This one is going around with a rather bad group, I'll either go with him or I'll get him to go some place else with me. This girl is being unjustly treated at work—over-worked or over-supervised. I'll speak to the boss about her and see what I can do about it. Week by week this goes on. Not only that, but week by week this is reported on. The following week, "Did you go out with that fellow?"—"Did you speak to the boss?" "What happened?" "Why or why not?" These people are serious about this, this is the Church in action today. They call this the "check up" and it goes on in any action they take, whether it be the action as a result of the social inquiry or possibly an action taken as a result of the religious inquiry or the Gospel inquiry, which is the same sort of study applied to a passage of the Gospel. This last is much shorter than the social inquiry but sometimes produces just as effective results.

In the YCW too the expression is also used, "review of influence." This is simply a report back on any other activities of the workers' life that might be of interest to their fellow workers. Any activity taking place in their workshop, any injustice, any good point they have seen. The review of influence might also consider activities of the group, socials that they are running, services such as services for the sick, employment services, dances, picnics and outings. The whole essence of the Movement consists in a constant and continual examination of the young worker's life, a checking on it, an improving of it, a planning to eliminate his problems and to give him anything that would help him reach Christ.

To see a well-trained YCW Section in operation is to understand why the various Holy Fathers have been so lavish in their praise of this particular form of the apostolate. Here is the Church of Christ as it touched modern industrialized, paganized reality. Here is the Church on the offensive, in the life of her children, a glorious Church, happy, integrated, generous, competent. A veritable army of the lay apostolate.

CHAPTER TWELVE

Queen of the Apostles

Of course, there is a Woman in the case. She is the fairest, loveliest, purest Woman of them all, Mary, the great Mother of God. All of the lay apostle's formation comes through her. Just as Christ came into the world through Mary, so the lay apostle is brought into his apostolate through her, the Queen of all apostles whether they be Bishops, priests or lay folk. "Woman behold they Son; Son behold thy Mother."

At first ordinarily the lay apostle does not understand this. He does not see Our Lady's role in his formation, her part in his apostolate. But it does dawn upon him gradually. Perhaps someone gives him St. Louis de Montfort's classic treatise, "True Devotion to the Blessed Virgin Mary." He starts it, maybe he's confused or even frightened, maybe it seems to him that Our Lady's role is a little exaggerated. He puts it aside for a while. "I'll go back to it later," he tells himself. That is fine.

As he continues in the apostolate gradually the lay apostle begins to think and hear more about Mary. Her role as the Mother of God—for the first time he sees the magnificence of this concept. Perhaps on a day of recollection someone talks about Mary Mediatrix of All Graces. He hears what perhaps he read in de Montfort and now he beings to comprehend—all graces come into the world through her as through a channel. He ties this up with his knowledge, also growing, of the Mystical Body and he suddenly realizes that she also plays a part in that Body. Christ is the Head, we the members, and she, as one of the Fathers of the Church pointed out, is the neck uniting the Head to the members.

Perhaps at this point the lay apostle learns something he has heard all his life and never understood, that Mary is the Co-Redemptrix of the human race. That Christ associated her with Him in the redemption of the world, that her suffering united with His suffering procured the salvation of the world—"Thou shalt lie and wait for her heel and she will crush they head." The apostolate continues through her. She helps supply the fruits of Calvary to each individual soul. Her diocese is the world entrusted to her by her Divine Son. His, the lay apostle's, is a tiny apostolate that can be effective only in and through the Queen of Apostles who has charge of all.

An apostolate in and through and with Our Lady cannot fail. Any other cannot exist. Her power with God is almost infinite. For this is she of whom the Book of Proverbs speaks and she to whom these words are applied by the Church in her Liturgy.

The Lord possessed me in the beginning of His ways, before He made anything, from the beginning. I was set up from eternity, and of old, before the earth was made. The depths were not as yet, and I was already conceived; neither had the fountains of waters as yet sprung out; the mountains with their huge bulk had not as yet been established; before the hills I was brought forth; He had not yet made the earth, nor the rivers, nor the poles of the world. When He prepared the heavens, I was there; when with a certain law and compass He enclosed the depths; when He established the sky above, and poised the fountains of waters; when He compressed the sea with its bounds, and set a law to the waters that they should not pass their limits; when He balanced the foundations of the earth; I was with Him, forming all things and was delighted every day playing before Him at all times; playing in the world; and my delight is to be with the children of men. Now therefore ye children, hear me: blessed are they that keep my ways. Hear instruction, and be wise, and refuse it not. Blessed is the man that heareth me, and that watcheth daily at my gates, and waiteth at the post of my doors. He that shall find Me shall find life, and shall have salvation from the Lord.

No one could ask for any more. No real lay apostle wants any less.

Selected Bibliography[1]

SPIRITUAL LIFE

Bellord, Rt. Rev. James, *Meditations on Christian Dogma* (Newman: Westminster, MD)

Boylan, Eugene, *This Tremendous Lover* (Newman: Westminster, MD)

Chautard, Dom, *The Soul of the Apostolate* (Kenedy: New York)

de Jaegher, Paul, *One with Jesus* (republished by Arouca Press)

—*Virtue of Trust* (Kenedy: New York)

de Montfort, Louis (St.), *True Devotion to the Blessed Virgin Mary*

de Sales, Francis (St.), *Introduction to the Devout Life*

Desplanques, François, *Living the Mass* (Newman: Westminster, MD)

Dohen, Dorothy, *Vocation to Love* (Sheed & Ward: New York)

Farrel, O.P., Walter, *A Companion to the Summa* (4 vols.) (Sheed & Ward: New York)

Garrigou-Lagrange, O.P., Reginald, *The Love of God and The Cross of Jesus* (Herder: St. Louis)

—*Three Ages of the Interior Life* (2 vols.) (Herder: St. Louis)

Gheon, Henri, *The Lives of the Saints* (Sheed & Ward: New York)

Gihr, Nicholas, *The Holy Sacrifice of the Mass* (Herder: St. Louis)

Houselander, Carol, *The Reed of God* (Sheed & Ward: New York)

Jarrett, O.P., Bede, *Meditations for Layfolk* (Burns, Oates: England)

---

[1] Many of these books are out-of-print but some have been republished.

Kempis, Thomas A, *The Imitation of Christ* (Harper Bros.: New York)

—(Sheed & Ward: New York)

—(Bruce Publishing: Milwaukee, WI)

Leen, C.S.Sp., Edward, *Progress in Mental Prayer* (Sheed & Ward: New York)

Marmion, Abbot, Columba, *Christ the Life of the Soul* (Herder: St. Louis, MO)

Plus, S.J., Raoul, *Radiating Christ* (The Grail: St. Meinrad's Abbey, IN)

—*Christ in Our Brethren* (The Grail: St. Meinrad's Abbey, IN)

Sheed, Frank J., *Map of Life* (Sheed & Ward: New York)

—*Society and Sanity* (Sheed & Ward: New York)

von Zeller, Dom Hubert, *We Die Standing Up* (Sheed & Ward: New York)

SPECIAL WORKS

Baptism Album — *Confirmation Album, Marriage Album, Mass Album* (Fides: Chicago, IL)

Holy Bible, especially the New Testament, numerous:

(Sheed & Ward: New York)

(St. Anthony Guild: Paterson, NJ)

St. Andrew's Daily Missal (E. M. Lohmann: St. Paul, MN)

CHURCH IN THE WORLD TODAY

Bishop, Clare Hutchet, *France Alive* (McMullin: New York)

de Montceuil, Yves, *For Men of Action* (Fides: Chicago, IL)

Perrin, S.J., Henri, *Priest Workman in Germany* (Fides: Chicago, IL)

Saliege, Cardinal, J.G., *Who Shall Bear the Flame?* (Fides: Chicago, IL)

Suhard, Cardinal, Emmanuel, *The Church Today* (Fides: Chicago, IL)

Trese, Leo, *Many Are One* (Fides: Chicago, IL)

van der Meersch, Maxine, *Fishers of Men* (Sheed & Ward: New York)

Ward, Maisie, *France Pagan* (Sheed & Ward: New York)

WOMAN

Faherty, S.J., W.B., *The Destiny of Modern Woman* (Newman: Westminster, MD)

Fitzsimons, John, *Woman Today* (Sheed & Ward: New York)

Vann, O.P., Gerald, *Eve and the Gryphon* (Newman: Westminster, MD)

MARRIAGE AND THE FAMILY

Buckley, Fr. Christian, *Designs for Sex* (Fides: Chicago, IL)

Hope, Winfield, *Life Together* (Sheed & Ward: New York)

Kelly, S.J., G., *Modern Youth & Chastity* (Queens Work: St. Louis, MO)

Sattler, C.SS.R., Henry, *Parents, Children and the Facts of Life* (St. Anthony Press: Paterson, NJ)

Vann, O.P., Gerald, *Christian Married Love* (Liturgical Press: St. John's Abbey, Collegeville, MN)

Willock, Ed, *Marriage for Keeps* (Integrity: New York)

—*Marriage and Birth* (Integrity: New York)

MARRIAGE AND THE FAMILY

Cardijn, Monsignor, Joseph, *The Church and the Young Worker* (Young Christian Workers, 638 W. Deming Pl., Chicago)

—*The Spirit of the Young Christian Workers* (Young Christian Workers, 638 W. Deming Pl., Chicago)

—*The Hour of the Working Class* (Young Christian Workers, 638 W. Deming Pl., Chicago)

Joseph, Rita, *The Worker and His Family* (Young Christian Workers, 638 W. Deming Pl., Chicago)

Priest Bulletin, *Priests' Bulletin* (Catholic Action Federation, 638 W. Deming Pl., Chicago)

MAGAZINES

America, 70 East 45th St., New York 17, NY

Commonweal, 386 Fourth Ave., New York 16, NY

Cross and Crown, Herder, St. Louis, MO

Integrity, 157 East 38th St., New York 16, NY

Jubilee, 377 Fourth Ave., New York 16, NY

The Catholic Mind, America Press, 70 East 45th St, New York City

PAPAL ENCYCLICALS AND ADDRESSES[2]

Leo XIII, *On the Condition of Labor*

Pius XI, *Reconstructing the Social Order*

Pius XII, *On the Mystical Body*

Pius XI, *On the Christian Marriage*

Pius XII, *Woman's Duties in Social and Political Life*

---

[2] These encyclicals and addresses can be found online.

Selected Bibliography

Pius XI, *On Atheistic Communism*

Pius XII, *The Lay Apostolate . . . It's Need Today*

Pius XII, *Christmas Message 1952*

Pius XII, *Democracy*